METHODS OF EARLY GOLF ARCHITECTURE

The Selected Writings of C.B. Macdonald,
George C. Thomas, and Robert Hunter

Presented by **Coventry House Publishing**

CONTENTS

CHAPTER 1

Characteristics of a Golf Architect

"A golf architect must be a student of agriculture, understand nature, have a knowledge of soils, knowledge of implements, drainage, and above all the particular character of the layout which tantalizes a lover of the game and holds him spellbound." – C.B. Macdonald

By C.B. Macdonald:

I do not think the term "golf architect" can be found in golf records previous to 1901, the time I formulated the ideas of copying the famous holes, sometimes not in their entirety; at times taking only some famous putting green or some famous bunker or some famous water hazard or other outstanding feature which might be adapted to particular ground over which one wanted to build a golf course. I believe this was the birth of golf architecture. Now golfing architecture has really become an art, and is so recognized, being akin to science. As artists, architects certainly should not be classified as golf professionals. A golf architect must be a student of agriculture, understand nature, have a knowledge of soils, knowledge of implements, drainage, and above all the particular character of the layout which tantalizes a lover of the game and holds him spellbound.

Architecture is one of the five fine arts. If the critic's contention is true, then architecture must be a "fetish," as the basis of it is the copying of Greek and Roman architecture, Romanesque and Gothic, and in our own times among other forms, Georgian and Colonial architecture. One must have the gift of imagination to successfully apply the original to new situations. Surely there is nothing "fetish" about this.

By George C. Thomas:

Above all things do not start with anyone who has not done such work before, and done it well, for those of us who have come through the fire of our own errors in golf construction realize how easily mistakes are made.

Many clubs have suffered from experimentation in golf construction.

Because a man has played golf well, has seen many courses, or even because he has, in addition, technical knowledge on other kinds of construction, it does not mean he can construct a golf course properly the first time he tries it.

———— ◆◆ ————

Therefore, do not fear to pay the price of a well-known golf architect, one who has worked at his craft for some years, and whose best reference is the reputation he has earned in nearby parts of your own district; for the golf course in a land of unknown conditions, is an unsolvable problem to a newcomer.

By Robert Hunter:

It would be absurd to think that we have one golf course architect capable of meeting and solving our many problems. I doubt if we shall ever have one capable of dealing successfully with such varying conditions as those which exist in Maine, in Florida, in Texas, in Colorado, and in California. Very soon, therefore, we should have schools to train for us architects, engineers, and green-keepers. Greenkeeping requires men with local experience. Trained men imported from the East, or from abroad, are rarely of much value in the Far West until they have spent a year or so in studying local conditions, or have learned valuable lessons by making costly and annoying mistakes. Yet our need is a crying one and should be emphasized on all possible occasions. Of first importance to any club undertaking to construct a golf course is a capable architect; but in meeting as best we may our many individual problems, let us not forget that the thing of first importance at present to the entire body of golfers in America is the training of first-rate architects, engineers, and greenkeepers. Until we have done this we shall continue to waste a large part of the immense sums we spend for golf.

———————•———————

To find the right man, really capable of designing and overseeing the construction of a golf course, is, of all things, the most important. But the ideal man is almost as difficult to find as the ideal terrain. There are few first-rate architects, and they are so busy that it is sometimes impossible to get the one most wanted. For some strange reason it is often thought that almost anyone can lay out and construct a golf course. As a result some clubs turn the task over to the leading amateur golfer of the community, the local professional, or anyone else who may offer himself as an architect. Such stupidity, more than anything else I know of, has been responsible for the incredible waste which has been so prevalent in most of the work in this field.

I do not know how much will be spent this year in America on new construction, but, if past experience is any guide, much of that money will be wasted, and at least an equal amount will later be spent on these courses in altering, obliterating, and rebuilding before the work is satisfactorily finished. If first-class architects were available to undertake all the new work, much of this money would be saved. Unhappily they are not available. The really capable men in golf course architecture could be named on the fingers of the two hands, and unless your course happens to be in the region where they have most of their work, I venture to say it will be almost impossible to obtain their services. Nevertheless, my most earnest advice to the members of any club undertaking to construct a course is this: if you seek something permanent, something that will give you real satisfaction and not be a heavy drag on your purse for many years, employ your architect only after careful inquiry, and get the best man obtainable regardless of his fee. There is a finality—that is the important thing—about the work of the best men which is worth tens of thousands to any club.

CHAPTER 2

Psychology of Design

"How deadly dull are two or three holes of the same character when they follow each other! A drive and pitch followed by a drive and pitch is a good deal like serving a watery pudding after a watery soup." – Robert Hunter

By C.B. Macdonald:

A golf hole, humanly speaking, is like life, inasmuch as one cannot judge justly of any person's character the first time one meets him. Sometimes it takes years to discover and appreciate hidden qualities which only time discloses, and he usually discloses them on the links. No real lover of golf with artistic understanding would undertake to measure the quality or fascination of a golf hole by a yardstick, any more than a critic of poetry would attempt to measure the supreme sentiment expressed in a poem by the same method. One can understand the meter, but one cannot measure the soul expressed. It is absolutely inconceivable.

By Robert Hunter:

It is not the love of something easy which has drawn men like a magnet for hundreds of years to this royal and ancient pastime; on the contrary, it is the maddening difficulty of it. One speaks of the masters, but who yet has mastered even its simplest detail? "It's a cruel sport," said its greatest master, Vardon, when he missed that famous putt which he or any child could have kicked in. But that is what fascinates man and leads him to leave business, home, wife, and children to pursue this hard mistress in the foolish hope of conquering her. What is more engaging than to see how golf infuriates some big brute who can thrash anybody, ride bucking horses, shoot deer on the run and birds on the wing! What is so delectable as to see him in a nervous tremor as he stands on the tee, glaring fiercely at that still, white little ball! How the game torments the adventurous soul, even him who with a bit of rag and a hollow shell defies wind and wave! Golf beats us all, and that is the chief reason we shall never cease loving her, nor ever give up our attempt to subdue her

————•◦•————

Great golfers would find the game stupid if no occasion arose to use the more difficult shots in their repertoire. The keenest delight in golf is given to those who, finding themselves in trouble, refuse to be depressed, and, with some recovery, snatch from their opponents what seemed for them certain victory. For the best golfers there are few really testing shots on even the most difficult of courses.

By George C. Thomas:
The strategy of the golf course is the soul of the game. The spirit of golf is to dare a hazard, and by negotiating it reap a reward, while he who fears or declines the issue of the carry, has a longer or harder shot for his second, or his

second and third on long holes; yet the player who avoids the unwise effort gains advantage over one who tries for more than in him lies, or who fails under the test.

—————•·•—————

On broken ground, hilly ground, or terrain with natural hazards, the golf architect must place his holes so that proper strategy is obtained from the natural topography. On flat, or fairly flat courses, he must place his hazards to take the place of natural ones, thereby attaining his purpose. There are innumerable ways and combinations to obtain this necessary finesse. Some are plainly evident from the tee, others will only be discovered after one plays near the green. Occasionally, your proper line will not become clear to you until you have gone over the hole a number of times. Such problems include the many diversities of carry from the tee, through the fairway and to the green, with the added artifices which may complicate the situation by the size and shape and levels of the green, and the numerous effects secured by dogleg holes, out of bounds, grades, winds, and divers other factors.

Every golfer can improve his game by playing for placement not only on his drive but through the fairway, and by trying to play for the point on the green which makes his putts easier. Years ago it was thought sufficient to play for the green, and if the golfer's shot reached it, he was satisfied. Then men came who played for the flag, and again, if near it, they were content. Now, as the game has developed, the best players try for the proper position near the pin, considering the slope of the ground so that they have the easiest putt, the uphill being easier than the downhill; the putt with the slope above at the right being simpler for most people than if the slope is above at your left, and so on.

VARIETY IN DESIGN

By Robert Hunter:

The spice of golf, as of life, lies in variety. A nine hole course full of variety will always be approached the second time with interest. But how deadly dull are two or three holes of the same character when they follow each other! A drive and pitch followed by a drive and pitch is a good deal like serving a watery pudding after a watery soup. Separate them sufficiently and each may be approached with some interest. Really good golf holes are full of surprises, each one a bit better than the last. Like a first-rate dinner, as soon as you have finished one course with beaming satisfaction something even better is placed before you. To arouse this zest each hole should have a character of its own. Its physiognomy should be quite distinct from that of its neighbors, and it should be one not easy to forget. Its personality should awaken your interest and cause you to question how best to approach it. It should present some problem to you in vivid form, and, even though that problem may be solved in two or three ways, it should be quite clear from the beginning that a choice must be made.

By C.B. Macdonald:

Variety is not only "the spice of life" but it is the very foundation of golfing architecture. Diversity in nature is universal. Let your golfing architecture mirror it. An ideal or classical golf course demands variety, personality, and, above all, the charm of romance.

HOME COURSE

By George C. Thomas:

In speaking of courses, each man believes that his own is far and away better than most others. He may admit his greens are poor, or that the trap on number six is badly placed or whatnot, but, nevertheless, he insists that outside of such minor things, his golf home is superior to most. He brings to mind the niblick shot he played in such and such a match; where else could that have been done? He saw Hagen take a 78 on his course, and no one can prove to him that they have a better layout at so and so. It is remarkable how this holds good. I know one course where there are more blind shots to the greens than at ten other places; yet, do you suppose the men who play that course think it poorer than others? They do not; they think it a fine test, all of which proves that there are many shots in golf, many thrills, the joy of overcoming varied difficulties; and to this is added home loyalty.

By C.B. Macdonald:

To my mind there is much nonsense preached regarding golf courses. It is not in my province to lay down the law—what is right or wrong—but so long as I am writing this story I am going to tell you what I think is best, regardless of any criticism there may be of it. Criticizing a golf course is like going into a man's family. The fond mother trots up her children for admiration. Only a boor would express anything else than a high opinion. So it is a thankless task to criticize a friend's home golf course. "Where ignorance is bliss 'tis folly to be wise." It is natural one should love his home course. He knows it, and with golf holes familiarity does not breed contempt, but quite the reverse.

This is best exemplified by experiences I have had in improving various holes on golf courses that I have fathered. Usually there is much objection to any alteration by the rank and file, but once done, when the club members become accustomed to the hole, they admit the justification for the alteration.

CHAPTER 3

Deciding Where to Build

"It is true that a group of golfers cannot always find an ideal terrain where they can build a fine golf course, but let the property be ever so flat, one may construct an interesting course." – C.B. Macdonald

By Robert Hunter:

The best land to purchase will be the first thing to engage the attention of a club. The importance of obtaining the right soil and sufficient acreage can hardly be overstressed. Many clubs, selecting their sites in haste, have never been able to correct their initial error. They have had to content themselves with mediocre golf or spend vast sums to increase their acreage and to modify the soil. In a few cases they have had to flee from the unconquerable, to buy a better site, and start all over again. One hears some tragic stories of what it has cost certain clubs to add a few acres to their original holdings in order to lengthen or to rearrange their courses. One club, starting with nine holes and buying its land for one hundred dollars an acre, was faced with the prohibitive price of ten thousand an acre for additional land. The saddest part of this story lies in the fact that had not the club made its neighborhood so attractive the land in that vicinity would have increased but little in value. The sorrowful fate of another club comes to mind. Having occasion to remodel a few holes it was found necessary to buy one additional acre. It had to pay twenty-five thousand for that acre, and several more thousand to blast away some tons of the solid stone of which this acre was composed. A wise club will, therefore, buy at the start a larger acreage than seems at the moment necessary for its requirements. If wisely chosen, the surplus land will one day yield a handsome profit.

———————●●———————

Do not go into hilly country if that can be avoided. Nearly all courses built in the hills are expensive to construct and tiresome to play. I know of no first-rate golf which requires hill climbing; nor can I recall one course which is popular with the membership. Shun also that country which is broken into many ravines. Such hazards are often quite picturesque, but they are rarely desirable and for the uncertain player they are fearful to look upon. Climbing in and out of canyons to retrieve balls is most exasperating, and on crowded days the play is so delayed as to prove a general nuisance. For the same reasons too many streams and ponds are objectionable. With the heavy ball now played no recovery shot is possible from water, and so long as this ball is in use it would seem wiser to keep as much as possible to those hazards from which shots can be played. In saying this, I do not forget the many charming holes in this country and abroad which are played over water; but one or two such holes in the eighteen will be quite enough.

What should be diligently sought for is land which resembles in character and contour links land. Here there are few abrupt or pronounced slopes, and yet the land is by no means flat. There are innumerable inequalities, gentle undulations, a continuous rising and falling of the surface, barely perceptible at times to the eye. It is true that even links land varies enormously. At Prince's and at St. George's one plays in and out of great swales lying between huge dunes, and now and then one is forced to cross the dunes. But at Deal, St. Andrews, Hoylake, and Westward Ho! one has the feeling of playing overly comparatively flat land. There is but little climbing and yet in the play one rarely finds the ball on an exact level with his feet. It is difficult to make clear to anyone who has not seen such land its unique character. To play golf there requires a great variety of strokes, and the placing of one's second shots amidst such undulations in a manner to make them serve on is a source of never ending delight. On the links the player has not only to deal with the formidable hazards, but also with countless little ones—those beautifully turfed, harmless looking undulations which run through the fairways from tee to green. Terrain of that sort will yield superlative golf anywhere.

If possible to avoid, do not select land with large outcroppings of rock, or with soil in which rock and gravel predominate. Such conditions will add greatly to the expense of construction. This is usually true also of land covered with timber. It is often difficult and very costly to remove stumps; and to put the land in good condition after that is done requires a lot of work. The soil in which pine delights to grow is often excellent for golf, and if the expense of clearing is not prohibitive a club will be wise to consider its possibility. Wholly flat land is rarely thought to be desirable for golf, and it is likely to be chosen only as a last resource. I am quite sure this is a mistaken view. Not only some of the most popular but some of the most interesting courses have been made of flat land. If the soil is desirable and sand can be readily obtained, some of the most attractive holes imaginable can be constructed on such land. As the greens can be placed anywhere, the layout in general should be without a flaw. The length of the holes will not be governed by certain situations which must be used, but will be decided by ideal considerations. With plough and scraper one can mold the surface at will, and create effects and problems which can but rarely be found provided by nature.

By George C. Thomas:

Many golf courses have been built in impossible locations, at additional cost of construction and upkeep.

In connection with soils, it is a question of ease of construction, of supplying drainage, and of ability to grow grass. Any location which gives these requisites is acceptable from the soil standpoint.

Properties will be found which contain deposits of sand. This is very valuable for many uses. Sometimes one finds leaf mold, which is helpful later for dressings of the greens; and, if possible, a tract which has these advantages should be secured.

The terrain is equally important with the soil. Anything from flat land, provided it can be drained, and will not be flooded by overflowing streams, to land without too great hills, may be properly considered golf territory. Heavy hills make the course too wearisome, and provide hazards from which it is impossible to recover.

Broadly speaking, where it is necessary to climb more than two steep hills and more than four medium grades, the course is approaching impracticability; and, speaking of hills, those should be considered heavy which require a climb of from seventy-five to one hundred feet or more; a medium grade one which is close to fifty feet. This is a perfectly arbitrary ruling, but is made after a study of the elevations to be surmounted on a number of courses.

———•◦•———

Beware of the man with land to sell who wishes you to build a golf course so that you can sell the land for him. Too often such a proposition brings conflicting interests into being and the course may suffer. Lay out your course first; do not skimp the rough between it and the lots to be sold later and after the course is completed; then, and not until then, build the subdivision. By such a careful method you will secure the maximum of golf value, use the minimum of land for your course, and develop the largest possible portion for sale without harming your layout.

CHAPTER 4

The Design Process

"The ability to create is to consider all the problems of a golf course. The architect must visualize the effect his work will produce from all angles of the game."
– George C. Thomas

By George C. Thomas:

After you have selected your architect and your location—and the former, if he does not aid in the choosing of the latter, should certainly pass upon it before purchase—you must have a frank and workable arrangement with your architect. This should not only be without possibility of misunderstanding from a business standpoint, but also as to the kind of course most desirable for your needs; the length of your course; the carries from the tees; your club's ideas of the trapping of the greens; of their construction, and other matters most necessary for you to program in advance—these should be thoroughly discussed and decided upon.

The well-conceived golf property must be designed as a whole; and while it is true that plans of the clubhouse and its necessary adjacent buildings, parking space, and so forth, should be worked out and submitted by the usual experts, nevertheless your golf architect must be consulted as to the situation of such units; for if they are not properly located they conflict with the course itself, and everything can be made to dovetail without interference.

Too often the site for the clubhouse is arbitrarily made, and the golf course must adapt itself to such selection. Many, many clubhouses are situated in locations which hamper the proper laying out of the course, and which are the cause of much discomfort to the playing membership.

One very common error is to place the clubhouse on the highest point of the property, which is often at a corner, making it very difficult to start and finish the course. Again, such a high point is at the end of a long, narrow strip of land, or located at the Western limit of the holdings, so that to return, the golfer must face the setting sun. Much criticism aimed at finishing holes is the fault of the clubhouse location rather than that of the golf architect.

———— •• ————

In the actual plan for the course, the greatest care must be taken to secure the full value, with the least congestion, moderate expense in construction and other necessary fundamentals.

The proper solution is much on the order of a chess problem; the first effort is not generally the best.

One must study the land and also the contour map before being able to commence work. Sometimes it seems as though the course worked itself out. One can readily see just where the holes will fit one after the other; but as a rule this is not the case, and the man who tries to walk over the ground once, and lay out the course as he goes, cannot expect to secure fine results. The starts and finishes should be worked out first. As one learns the land and its possibilities, one commences to visualize greens, tee shots, and even entire fairways, which appear here and there disjointedly, just as one discovers parts of a picture puzzle which stand out clearly, but do not fit with any other pieces already patched together. Such finds should be sketched on a map for future reference.

Among the green sites which stand out are some which are too fine to lose, and other holes must be discovered which will link them together. When you are able to so connect several holes with a start or finish, you are beginning to place the framework of your golf course.

Soon you have before you a part of a nine, and the puzzle is to bring this into touch with your finish and your start of the same nine. Here it is that the one-shot holes are so valuable, because one-shotters aid you in welding the disconnected links of your golf chain.

Too often you must either give up one promising hole or another, as you will frequently find it impossible to bring these together; and to arrive correctly at your solution you should work out problems on your contour map and on paper, and decide which has the most superlative worth. Unless the solution comes with reasonable quickness on the ground, you will soon be marking up maps at a great rate, and a little trick taught me by Willie Tuckie, Jr., is a wonderful aid. Your map is, of course, contoured to scale, and you can cut out of blotting paper miniature fairways, making them also to the same scale as the map; it is easy to place them on your contour map with thumb tacks, first having your map on a board.

You will find that by hinging these little fairways at or about the two hundred-yard mark, you can make them follow the contours on the map as doglegs or straight holes. You can play with them just as if they were picture puzzle units; and by making them of different lengths, all to scale, with their width corresponding to that of fairways from sixty-five to eighty yards wide, the one-shotters unhinged and the three-shot holes hinged twice, you will find them of the utmost help.

Such a plan gives you clear thinking as you work on your map, and avoids constantly using new maps or erasing lines already drawn and found useless.

The contour map is of the greatest assistance, but the ground must be checked with it, the locations carefully marked and oriented both on the ground and on the map with exactness and agreement.

By Robert Hunter:

Next after the question of routing—and it will surely be wise not to follow St. Andrews in that—comes the problem of length. Unless the club has definitely decided to depart from well-established standards, the eighteen holes should have a total length of at least six thousand yards. Even then it will be wise to provide, wherever possible, for adding length in case it should later be required. The longest courses these days are about sixty-eight hundred yards, and it is impossible to foresee what the ultimate limits are to be. If each year the manufacturers add length to the ball, it will be necessary, if we wish to maintain a championship standard, to provide for extending our courses also indefinitely. In judging the plans of your architect, it is well to have clearly in mind whether or not you wish to enter the race for yardage. It is a difficult question. Some of the best courses in this country and abroad are the short ones. The most famous in Great Britain is at North Berwick, and I am quite sure that most good golfers would rather play there than on many long, tiresome, featureless courses with a thousand more yards.

The thing to seek above everything else is a course offering to the players many problems of interest and a few holes of the highest quality. These are the reasons for the enduring popularity of North Berwick. With no little irritation, I have watched architects struggling desperately to get yardage and, in order to get it, sacrificing without compunction holes of real quality. I have seen fine two-shot holes ruined by putting back the tees in order to make holes of five hundred yards, although not one in fifty of that length awakens in the player the slightest interest. I have seen designers stretching out holes to three hundred yards—another length out of which holes of quality are rarely made. What would the world think if some such stupidity should turn the Redan into a drive and pitch? The architects have done many absurd things in order to get yardage, but the blame does not wholly rest upon them. That the par of a hole should depend upon its length is in part responsible, but the long flying ball now manufactured is the chief culprit. A hole of about six hundred yards will occasionally be reached by two of Mitchell's best shots, and these days there are other hitters of almost equal power. Of course the ball has made such distances possible, and unless some regulation is devised, the ball will force us on and on in this mad race for yardage. It is playing the Bolshevik with our golf courses— undermining old standards and forcing us to destroy annually a great deal of valuable property.

It is interesting to observe that the "King's," which is the long course at Gleneagles, measures only sixty-three hundred and forty yards. It has five one-shot holes, and no hole over four hundred and fifty-five yards in length. Its difficulty lies in the testing short holes, and in the large number of very fine two-shot holes. I am printing below a table of American courses of the first class, giving the yardage in each case:

Club	Yardage
The National	6,163
Midwick	6,300
Brookline	6,350
Los Angeles	6,390
Engineers'	6,400
Myopia	6,400
Essex County	6,410
Garden City	6,417
Mayfield	6,440
Pine Valley	6,446
San Francisco	6,462
Flossmoor	6,475
Detroit	6,502
Merion	6,515
Inverness	6,569
Ojai	6,625
Lido	6,693
Oakmont	6,707

Passing from these questions of length we arrive at one principle which can be stated in positive terms. The first and second nines should balance each other in yardage and character. The second nine should never be shorter and easier to play than the first. That would be in the nature of an anticlimax. Indeed, the last few holes should be the most difficult in the round. One should be in form to play his best golf then, and in all matches the last three or four holes should have to a high degree the quality of taking the measure of the players, and awarding the prize to the one most deserving.

By C.B. Macdonald:

In discussing and comparing the merits of the various courses, one is struck immediately with the futility of argument unless some basis of excellence is agreed upon, premises on which to anchor. In view of this, I have tried to enumerate all the essential features of a perfect golf course in accordance with the enlightened criticism of today, and to give each of these essential characteristics a value, the sum total of which would be 100, or perfection. Following is the result:

1. Course
    (a) Nature of the soil: 23
    (b) Perfection in undulation and hillocks: 22
    Total: 45
2. Putting greens
    (a) Quality of turf: 10
    (b) Nature of undulation well placed: 5
    (c) Variety: 3
    Total: 18
3. Bunkers and other hazards
    (a) Nature, size, and variety: 4
    (b) Proper placing: 9
    Total: 13
4. Length of hole

(a) Best length of holes: 8
(b) Variety and arrangement of length: 5
Total: 13
5. Quality of turn of fairgreen: 6
6. Width of fairgreen of the course 45 to 60 yards: 3
7. Nature of teeing ground, proximity to putting green: 2
Total: 100

DESIGN FLAWS

By George C. Thomas:

There are many glaring errors seen on most of our courses, and one of the commonest mistakes is to have a green with a wide opening in front of it, and difficulties nearby, especially beyond the green, or at its far sides; for a man who has fallen short of the green is thereby enabled easily to run his ball up to the pin, whereas the man who has made a bold stroke, possibly landing on the green with his ball, and running over the green, is given a more difficult lie after a finer effort. To offset this situation, it is advisable in many cases where there are long second shots to a green, to make a fairway beyond the green, so that the man who goes over has at least as good a chance to play back and near the hole as the man who falls short after an indifferent stroke.

This difficulty is overcome to some extent by trapping short of the green, but such hazards must not be too close where a long shot is necessitated, unless there is sufficient room beyond.

By Robert Hunter:

In order to get the standard length for the full eighteen we are also committing some stupid blunders. That we must have a course of at least sixty-three hundred yards is becoming a fixed idea. Such courses are referred to sometimes as courses of championship caliber, as if length alone were sufficient to qualify in that class. Not infrequently, as a matter of fact, quality is sacrificed in order to get length. I have seen a number of fine holes ruined by putting back the tees. One of the best two-shot holes I know was converted into nothing whatever by putting back the tee a hundred yards. Another magnificent hole—a one-shotter—was converted into less than nothing by making it three hundred yards in length. There is nothing of more credit to a course than to have holes of a proper length; and while this is something difficult to obtain and to keep, so long as the ball played with is changing from day to day, there are certain distances which can rarely be made to yield good golf. Sometimes an architect will stretch out his holes just far enough to increase their par value, and make the three shots of the mediocre player about as serviceable as the two big ones, and the chip made by the long player.

———•———

There are more mistakes made in constructing the hazards than anywhere else in building golf courses. There are deep traps to catch the drive and shallow traps to catch the second, when the reverse should be the practice. At the back of some greens, calling for a full wood, I have seen formidable hazards exacting cruel penalties for a superb shot a bit too strong. I well remember one such trap with banks so perpendicular that one has occasionally to play one shot away from the green, and another back on to the green. Only a lunatic will play a bold second at that hole. One sees no end of traps with regular lines, perpendicular sides, and sharp angles at the comers. In many places in such traps the best of golfers will sometimes find his ball in an almost unplayable position. Those bunkers are countless which have steep angular "cops" which can only be cut by a sickle. What a rare collection of weeds is always to be found in such places! We have all seen traps built on such pronounced slopes that every rain washes away all their sand, and we have seen others so opened to the wind that every stiff breeze sweeps them clean.

By C.B. Macdonald:

Motoring to Southampton, I pass a goodly number of new courses. As I view the putting greens it appears to me they are all built similarly, more or less of a bowl or saucer type, then built up toward the back of the green, and then scalloped with an irregular line of low, waving mounds or hillocks, the putting green for all the world resembling a pie-faced woman with a marcel wave. I do not believe anyone ever saw in nature anything approaching these homemade putting greens. Then scattered over the side of the fairway are mounds modeled after haycocks or chocolate drops. The very soul of golf shrieks!

———•————

Viewing the monstrosities created on many modern golf courses which are a travesty on Nature, no golfer can but shudder for the soul of golf. It would seem that in this striving after "novelty and innovation," many builders of golf courses believe they are elevating the game. But what a sad contemplation!

———•————

Before closing I wish to enumerate a few defects which unavoidably exist on some really good courses:

More than three blind holes are a defect and they should be at the end of a fine long shot only. Excessive climbing is a detriment. Mountain climbing is a sport in itself and has no place on a golf course. Trees in the course are a serious defect, and even when in close proximity prove a detriment. Out of bounds should be avoided if possible. Cops are an abomination. Glaring artificiality of any kind detracts from the fascination of the game.

CHAPTER 5

Utilizing Natural Features

"Now and then one finds a hole of real distinction which nature herself has modeled, and to add anything artificial would be a crime." – Robert Hunter

By Robert Hunter:

When we build golf courses we are remodeling the face of nature, and it should be remembers that *the greatest and fairest things are done by nature and the lesser by art*, as Plato truly said. Of nearly all golf course building at present and of nearly all landscape gardening for centuries, Plato's observation is strikingly true. What garden in all the world equals some of the pictures which nature paints? What modern golf course equals in beauty the seaside courses, especially those which have been left freest from the touch of the architect? If there has been improvement in the art of constructing golf courses, it has been largely due to the willingness of the best architects to imitate humbly and lovingly what nature has placed before them

Natural hazards are almost always beautiful, and those which are built, whether they be depressions cut in the surface or mounds raised above ground, may be made no less so. All artificial hazards should be made to fit into the ground as if placed there by nature. To accomplish this is a great art. Indeed, when it is really well done, it is—I think it may truly be said—a fine art, worthy of the hand of a gifted sculptor. They should have the appearance of being made with the same carelessness and abandon with which a brook tears down the banks which confine it, or the wind tosses about the sand of the dunes. In nature, rock, tree roots, and turf bind the soil, and when wind or water assails it, the less resistant portions give way, forming depressions or elevations broken into irregular lines.

By George C. Thomas:

In golf construction art and utility meet; both are absolutely vital; one is utterly ruined without the other. On the artistic side there is a theory of construction with a main fundamental that we copy nature; in this all seem to agree. There are minor exceptions which are permitted, as the placing of sand traps in a country otherwise devoid of sand; the cutting of fairway and green with uncut surroundings; the planting of varied trees, shrubs, and grasses which do not always blend with existing conditions, and the practical necessity of including fittings and implements required in the general scheme of upkeep and play.

The contours of our tees, of our hazards, of our greens, of our rough, and of our fairways should, except when otherwise absolutely necessary, all melt into the land surrounding them, and should appear as having always been present. The washing of water makes smooth, gradually fading lines, as, for example, the sand bar; and the soft, rolling curves of low, gently rounded hills are most attractive if copied in our molding. Where we have natural washes, many of their lines fade imperceptibly, and float or vanish into other contours with which they come in contact. Such flowing, graceful curves are very valuable in the artificial contouring or modeling of approaches to greens, of greens themselves, and of mounds adjacent; also for the sides, backs, and fore parts of hazards.

<hr />

While easy lines are beautiful and pleasing, they are not the only things we need in our golf architecture from the artistic point of view; and as a matter of utility they are not satisfactory if used alone. Variety must again be considered. We must have a contrast to orient our curving rolls, for not only will it make them prominent, but will aid whatever point we desire in fairway carry or green carry, or green entrance, and most of all of the green itself, to stand out to the view of the golfer. If we blend everything, nothing is accentuated, and in golf the position in which the ball should be placed must be emphasized, and the ability of the player to visualize or focus the distance to such a spot, by aid of our contrasts, is the supreme test of our work. The flat plain, with a flag on a flat green, cannot be oriented, neither can gently blending lines be conspicuous.

For this reason we need sharper and sterner patterns for proper visibility, and we have much in nature to copy. There are the tops of sand dunes gashed by ocean winds, where the sand that once held a curve has slipped away. There are irregular shapes caused by erosion, where water has undermined land, and the overhanging bank presents rough edges amidst the curves. We have hills with jagged slopes, and there are many contrasts in nature made by other forces than those which created the flowing forms, and these have union with our easy rolls.

CHAPTER 6

---·-·---

Teeing Grounds

"A good architect can always be distinguished from his less talented colleagues by the manner in which he builds his tees and by his cleverness in placing them."
– Robert Hunter

By Robert Hunter:

For some unaccountable reason the tees on many golf courses seem to have been given no thought whatever. How frequently on courses with some pretensions we see wretched tees, sadly neglected, badly placed, and insufficient in size! The matter of upkeep is beyond my purpose here, but the size and placement of the tees are vital problems in construction. The first and most important point to have in mind in building tees is to make them wherever possible indistinguishable from a fine bit of the fairway. Do not raise them above the level of the fairway unless there is real need for doing so. If they are raised, do the work on a big scale so that the rise and fall will be almost imperceptible. A good architect can always be distinguished from his less talented colleagues by the manner in which he builds his tees and by his cleverness in placing them. I have seen many an indifferent hole made into one of real quality merely by shifting the tee. I have seen short holes transformed from something trivial and insignificant into something of note by the same method. Some mediocre courses could, I am sure, be made into something quite creditable if some first-rate man were employed to select better positions for their tees.

In the case of the tees as in that of the greens the placement should often be at an angle with the center of the fairway. A good deal of yardage is lost on certain courses by forcing the players to walk thirty or forty yards to the right or left in order that the tee shall line up with the center of the next fairway. This happens almost always on those dreadful courses with a series of parallel holes. All such courses would be vastly improved by placing the tees as near as possible to the greens, and by playing at an angle to the center of the fairway. Most holes are improved by introducing a slight bend in the line of play; and the interest of the tee shot is increased because most players will be tempted to shorten the line to the hole by keeping as close as possible to the margin of the fairway. The interest at the short holes will also be intensified by building several different tees at varying distances and angles from the green.

Building several tees for most of the holes is the most economical way yet found to give variety to the play, and the only way available often to make certain holes attractive and testing for all classes of players. Moreover, it is the only way by which it is possible to maintain the par value of some holes in all winds and weather. A strong head wind which takes thirty or forty yards off the shot will often ruin fine two-shot holes, unless there is a forward tee for such occasions. A hole with cross hazards for the drive or the second shot is often converted into a wretched three-shot hole by certain winds. To be forced to play short of such hazards is most irritating to those players who realize that a forward tee for such winds would have made the play on such a day more thrilling than ever. It is, I think, a sound practice to build several tees on certain holes so that their length may be diminished when adverse wind or weather is certain to add a stroke in the play.

By George C. Thomas:

Tees should never obtrude, and, where possible, they may be part of the fairway. Yet, sometimes it is expedient to build them separately, and they should lose themselves, if practicable, as much as other artificial moldings, into contacting topography.

Raised tees require more water in dry conditions and are unsightly, but aid utility where, because raised, they give a better view of the shot to be played; and so raised, their boundaries should, of course, fade gradually into the ground near them.

————◄►————

For club courses, with large playing memberships, and an average of from one hundred to one hundred and fifty a day, tee surfaces for holes on which wood is used from the tee should be not less than two thousand square feet at a minimum; twenty-five hundred would be a better area, and three thousand square feet ample provision. On such courses for tees needing iron shots, a larger area is required; twenty-five hundred square feet should be a minimum of surface. If several tees are used, put five-eighths of your area for the central tee; one-quarter for the back, or championship tee, and one-eighth for the short tee location.

For smaller courses, where the average play would not exceed fifty a day, it would be advisable to use not less than half the maximum space figured for the larger courses, because, as a rule, clubs with a small playing membership desire the ultimate of perfection in upkeep.

———•◦•———

In connection with tees, where there is a prevailing wind, the regular tee will soon be ascertained, but if the prevailing wind changes to the opposite direction, the value of the hole is at once altered, and the greenkeeper should be instructed to use his long tees when there is a following wind, and when there is a very strong, adverse wind, to use the front of his middle tee, or possibly to advance his markers to the most forward starting place. For the same reason, with a heavy cross wind, the markers may be changed, and by such placing of the markers, and the use of the tees, the proper value of course strategy is maintained.

From the back tee of a course with several tees, the carry should be from one hundred and sixty five to one hundred and ninety yards, depending, of course, upon various conditions, such as the prevailing wind and the fact that the hazard may be above the tee, under which condition the distance across the hazard should be reduced. From the center tee the carry should roughly be, under average conditions, from one hundred and forty to one hundred and sixty five yards, and from the short tee one hundred and twenty yards is maximum distance. All measurements should be made from the center of the tee, and where there is a dogleg, the distance of the holes should be taken from the middle of the fairway. The angle of the dogleg should be considered as from two hundred to two hundred and fifty yards, depending on conditions which affect the length of the shot. On some holes there need be no carry from the tee, forced or optional; but here the drive must be placed accurately, and good distance required on it to make the second shot easier or reasonably possible. To develop this theory too far, and omit carries, one would lose diversity; and, in addition, the thrill of seeing your well-hit ball from the tee soar strong and true over a hazard is a thing not to be too often lost.

By C.B. Macdonald:

I should always advise a place for three tees; one the championship tee, which would probably give pleasure to less than five percent of your club membership; then the regular tees, which two-thirds of your club membership really care to play, leaving about thirty percent of your club membership to play from the short tees, which means men who can drive only about one hundred and twenty or one hundred and thirty yards. This gives all your members a fair game and you do not take the joy out of their life.

CHAPTER 7

Through the Green

"I believe in reverencing anything in the life of man which has the testimony of the ages as being unexcelled, whether it be literature, paintings, poetry, tombs—even a golf hole." – C.B. Macdonald

By George C. Thomas:

In the matter of fairways the amount of traffic must be taken into account, because narrow fairways cause congestion; but, as a general rule, fairways should average from sixty-five to eighty yards in width for the reception of long tee shots.

Although it is very often advisable to provide fairway immediately in front of tees, the first hundred yards should not be cut short as is the main body of the fairway. Frequently, there will be rough ground in front of the tee which should not be touched, but the short player should not have much over one hundred yards of ordinary rough to negotiate. At one hundred yards from the tee, a width of forty yards for the fairway is ample. The width of the fairway should then increase up to one hundred and eighty yards from the tee, where it should have its greatest width. It should remain at this width to two hundred and fifty yards, after which, on a two-shotter, it may gradually decrease to the green; it should not exceed the green entrance unless on holes requiring exceptionally long shots to the green.

On three-shot holes the fairway should be kept at good width after reaching one hundred and eighty yards, until within short range of the green, where it should be narrow, except that on the few very long three-shotters, where a long third is required to the green for perfect play, there should be fairways at the sides and back of the green. As in other matters, the location of your fairway near the green depends on the kind of shots which will be played to that green.

On many courses there are found unnecessarily wide fairways which increase the cost of upkeep.

On dogleg holes the fairway should be wider at the angle of the dogleg, and, as with greens, the width of fairways should be governed by the shots they are designed to accommodate.

Island fairways provide strategy where the ball must be played over rough to secure an advantageous position before a chance at the green is obtainable. The island fairway has many attractive variations, but is not adaptable in a clay country with a long, dry season and artificial irrigation, where the rough has speed without vegetation. The fourth hole at Lido, Long Island, is a splendid example of an island fairway with a safe route for the average player.

The cutting of the sides of fairways should not be made in straight lines, for, as noted by numerous writers, the curves made by the edges of fairways enable players and caddies to mark more easily balls which go in the rough. Lately, on a number of courses where rough has no outstanding features, painted stakes have been placed so that balls may be more readily marked.

----------◄►----------

The rough includes all low growth, and it is necessary, but often severe. The lost ball feature of rough is an ever-present evil. Much country will supply its own rough, and the natural is often as good as, or better than, the artificial, and it is adapted to the prevailing climatic conditions; but rough should always be modified, if too heavy, so that it is generally possible to get the ball back on the fairway in a properly executed stroke.

Long grass should not be too long. Other kinds of rough may be thinned here and there. Rocky ground should be picked over and improved; and no rough should be so severe that, as a rule, several strokes must be tried before a player is able to recover, or that recovery is almost impossible. This, of course, does not apply to water hazards, or to canyons in a country without rain, which are treated as water hazards under the rules.

As bad as unfairly severe rough is rough which gives no penalty, the worst type of which is hard, bare ground where the topped ball runs fast and far, and from which it is easy to play a long recovery shot by use of jigger or well-lofted shallow spoon. Such improper rough is often found on clay soil in a country which requires irrigation for its fairways in summer, and where the unwatered land at the side of the fairway has become baked, and is practically without growth. The remedy is the planting of trees staggered along the edge of such rough, with occasional sand traps, and, if possible, watering.

----------◄►----------

Rolls or ridges short of a green are valuable in some cases, but are difficult to cut, and dry out badly in heated conditions. They are only practical in damp climates, unless they may be sprinkled under dry conditions; and one of the most objectionable sights on a golf course is the dried out mounds and rolls which have not been watered. This applies to all types of rolls, including those which are part of the framework of a hazard.

Nevertheless, rolls with sufficient width for their height do not dry out easily and are most interesting as hazards; and in addition to such artificial ridges which affect the course of the ball, natural rolls or slopes should be taken advantage of for the same purpose.

A ball hitting on a down slope which slants toward the fairway from either side will secure a longer run, and, therefore, greater distance—unless the fairways are soggy—than the ball striking the flat fairway. All such runs afford fine strategy, for when the slope is near the rough or traps, the player takes considerable risk in trying to place his ball on it to secure the additional distance, while such traps are out of the way of the short player.

APPROACH SHOTS

By Robert Hunter:

There is no portion of a golf course which requires more care at the time of construction, and more attention later in the upkeep, than the area upon which most approaches to the hole will land. What decisive and subtle influences may be made to work upon the ball at just this point! By cleverly molding this area, what fine shots may be called forth! It is just here where some of the seaside courses outclass all others. Those gentle undulations and oblique ridges which often lie just at the opening of the greens in links land, force the golfer to use his head and all the skill at his command. Pulls or slices, runs or cuts, high balls or low balls may be required to overcome their insidious and artful purposes. Now and then, it is true, they close the door to the wayward who has not come to them by the straight and narrow path, and he must play some silly little shot to get back into the proper position. Problems of this sort may easily be overdone. Most of the areas in front of a green should be level and true; but there are holes where slight ridges, little swales and swells, the latter often barely raising their heads, may be used to call forth a variety of fine shots. Most balls receive their final touch at this point, yet how often we see courses where the approaches have not only been overlooked by the architect, but also forgotten by the greenkeeper. They are sometimes rough and uneven. At other times they are nurseries for weeds and coarse grasses which menace, and in time destroy, whatever good turf may linger on the neighboring greens. The climax of golf is at the hole, and the molding and care of the entrance to the green is of no less importance than of the green itself.

By George C. Thomas:

If the architect properly visualizes the way the golf ball will act, his green should retain the well played shot, and the poor shot should either fall short of the green or go beyond it or to the sides, making a par more difficult.

It cannot be emphasized too strongly, that the area of the green, and all the factors of rough and hazard adjacent, must work into the strategy of the hole. The tee shot must require certain placements in areas of proper surface, and the green must require more exact placements to areas of balanced surface.

In this connection, pitches should require distance rather than direction, because pitches are played by clubs with considerable loft, and shots from such clubs are more difficult to keep on the exact line than shots from clubs with less loft.

The running shots, on the contrary, are usually played from clubs with slight loft, and require direction rather than exact distance.

In conformity with this, pitch-and-run shots, which are approximately halfway between the pitch shot and the running shot, should demand reasonable direction and reasonable distance.

For these reasons short, or fairly short pitch shots should have greens built for their reception which have little depth and extreme width, and a trap close in front of the green; while for running shots, the green with great depth and narrow width, with traps at the sides of the opening, is advisable. For the medium pitch-and-run, the green with nearly equal width and depth is the requisite.

It will be seen from these suggestions that the guide for green surfaces is made not only for flat conditions, but also for the average medium-high shot to the green; and that, where the architect forces the player to make a certain type of shot to a green, his green must conform in depth and width, and total surface to the shot exacted.

———————◄•►———————

Lately it has been found an advance to make fairways beyond the green itself, instead of having mounds or rough behind the green. By placing rolls from twenty to fifty feet beyond the back of the green, one gives a chance for the reasonable return play of the ball which goes over the green; and the mounds a little further back give as much orientation as if closer, while the extra fairway supplies room for the long shot and reduces the expense of upkeep of large green surfaces.

Such a fairway beyond the green must not be made for very exacting shots, unless you have an opening for the short player which requires a long shot for the green, and on this angle you can give fairway beyond the green; whereas on the line of the long player this fairway should not be made if his shot will be a pitch. This may be accomplished by having a long, narrow green opening up for the shot of the short man on one side of the fairway, and a trap placed beyond his drive's reach, yet arranged to catch the drive of the long hitter, and which he cannot carry; this will penalize a topped second shot of the short man. On the other side of the fairway the long man, by a fine carry, has his pitch shot to the flag.

CHAPTER 8

———————•ı•———————

Hazards

"The object of a bunker or trap is not only to punish a physical mistake, to punish lack of control, but also to punish pride and egotism." – C.B. Macdonald

By Robert Hunter:

Without well-placed hazards, golf would fail to arouse and to satisfy man's sporting instincts. Hazards—how well chosen the name! They are risks; and penalties must come to those who take risks and fail. One may take a chance—or place a hazard on the turn of a card, and, if fortune favors, one wins; but when one takes a hazard at golf, skill and not luck will be the cause of his winning. Nothing ventured, nothing gained, is particularly true of golf; but he who overestimates his powers and takes wild chances is more of a gambler than a golfer. Hazards make golf dramatic; and the thrills that come to one who ventures wisely and succeeds are truly delectable. Without hazards golf would be but a dull sport, with the life and soul gone out of it. No longer would it attract the lusty and the adventurous, but would be left to those who favor insipid perambulation, suited to the effeminate and the senile.

———————•ı•———————

There can be no real golf without hazards, and unless these be varied, plentiful, and adroitly placed there will be no great golfers. Hazards are the decisive influence in the making of golfers. They fashion the shots of the youth. Let the greens be well-guarded and the youth will soon learn to pitch and stop. With undulations before him, he will become an adept at placing his shots—whether pitching or running. Build pits on the borders of the fairways and he will learn to keep down the middle, and give him a few heroic carries to make and the results will be all that can be desired. In the old days one could often tell whence a golfer came by the shots he had. The product of St. Andrews could rarely pitch well, but his running shots were marvelous to behold. Not infrequently he was a wild hitter of good length, that being a rather profitable ball at St. Andrews, where many of the bunkers lie in the middle of the fairways. At Sandwich the shots of most of the golfers have a fine carry, that being an essential there. In this manner are golfers fashioned by the courses they play on. The placing of the hazards and the molding of the greens force players to develop those shots which are found most effective in meeting the problems presented.

————————

In placing hazards, one should always have clearly in mind what one desires to accomplish. Unless they have some well-defined purpose, hazards may often be a cause of annoyance without in the least improving the golf or increasing the interest in the play. If it is the desire of the architect merely to punish faulty play, let him determine before placing a hazard what class of players is most likely to suffer. It is better not to punish the majority of bad shots as they are in themselves sufficient punishment.

Nearly every shot of certain players is a misfortune, and to set ourselves the task of adding to their misery is as cruel as it is unnecessary. Our task is rather to find ways of letting these wayward individuals have as much margin as possible, while at the same time protecting the greens in such a manner that whatever punishment the players receive will appear to have been brought upon them by their own errors. There are, however, times when in order to preserve the quality of a hole, we must deal harshly with all offenders. I am thinking, for instance, of a hole where a topped mashie shot may run dead to the pin, and of those down grades where a topped drive may result in a longer ball than one which has been truly hit. I am also reminded of those long pulls and slices on holes of medium length, where, if there are no traps, the wayward ball may be quite as well off as the good one. In such cases bad shots must be punished, otherwise there will be no reward for merit. The purpose of such hazards is to exact a penalty, and to place them properly is not a difficult matter.

Other hazards must often be placed to protect tees, greens, clubhouses, tennis courts, and so on. Still other hazards are sometimes required to protect the players from paying too great a penalty for bad shots—to prevent balls from going out of bounds, rolling down steep hills, or into swamps and ravines. The conditions which govern the placing of such hazards vary with each club and almost any experienced golfer may be trusted to establish their position. As they are planned in all such cases for protection they should, of course, be effective, but they should not be more severe than is necessary to accomplish this purpose. In fact, penalties wherever exacted should never be so severe as to make a recovery of some sort impossible. Nothing seems to me more out of place on a golf course than those areas from which no shot can be played, such as deep unkempt ravines, swamps, etc. Some designers have a passion for placing their tees at the edge of areas of that sort. The duffer is, of course, terrified when facing such hazards, and his wretched shots are cruelly punished. On the other hand, the scratch player seldom sees them, and only his rare shots which are completely missed will be penalized. By doing stupid things of that sort some golf course architects have created so much antagonism that even to mention the profession in some clubs is to lay one's self open to abuse.

By George C. Thomas:

It has been an old saying, and quoted in a number of books, that "no hazard which is visible is unfair"—or words to that effect—and most certainly every carrying hazard should be visible except under some special condition. Therefore, place your hazards on slight rises, if possible, which makes them more natural, without additional work; and if high spots are not in the right locations you must build your hazards above the surrounding ground, so that they may be seen and oriented. It is always advisable to show at least some little patch of sand above the surrounding ground level in order that the golfer may observe it from most positions; and it is remarkable how a little gleam of sand throws out its environment by virtue of contrast.

Notwithstanding the old saying regarding the fairness of visible hazards, the writer believes that many hazards are unfair because they are unnecessary and not contained in the strategy of the hole. To penalize without method is certainly improper; and carries which give no alternative line but the wearisome process of playing short, border on injustice and rightfully cause criticism.

———————●●———————

Water hazards are among the best and most thrilling of natural strategy, and sometimes artificial water hazards are well conceived. Like everything else, such trouble should not be overdone. Diversity, and yet again, variety, is the spice of a golf course. If one could have a course with sand dunes, with water hazards both as streams and as lakes, with fairways through virgin forests, with long, rolling contours, high plateaus, lovely little valleys to play through and to cross as hazards, one would have the superlative and ideal golf country. Such is Pine Valley, laid out by the master hand of that sterling sportsman, George Crump. Every true golfer loves Pine Valley—It may be censured by some as very difficult, especially recovery from the rough; yet its charm is the lure of diversity coupled with the thrill of surmounting its varied hardships.

By C.B. Macdonald:

The only thing that I do now is to endeavor to make the hazards as natural as possible. I try not to make the course any harder, but to make it more interesting, never forgetting that eight percent of the members of any golf club cannot, on an average, drive more than one hundred and seventy five yards, so I always study to give them their way out, permitting them without having to negotiate unsurmountable difficulties to reach the green, by taking a course much as a yachtsman does against an adverse wind, by tacking. To my mind this is a fundamental in golf course construction.

———————●●———————

The undulations and the run of the ball tell the story as to how the hazards should be placed. Don't place them without experience. Generally speaking, they should be of great variety, the greater the better, but always fair. By fair I mean where a player can extract the ball in one shot if reasonably well played in some direction.

Errors in play should be severely punished in finding hazards, but now the golfer wants his bunkers raked and all the unevenness of the fairway rolled out. A player does not get the variety of stances or lies that in olden times one was sure to have. A hanging lie or a ball lying in any position other than level is a blemish to the modern golfer. The science and beauty of the game is brought out by men having to play the ball from any stance. To play the game over a flat surface without undulations leaves nothing to the ingenuity of the player, and nothing is presented but an obvious and stereotyped series of hits. Today there seems to be a constant endeavor to make golf commonplace, to emasculate it, as it were, of its finer qualities.

BUNKERS

By Robert Hunter:

There is a much-quoted saying that no bunker which can be seen is a bad bunker. And this means, I suppose, that if you can see a bunker you have only yourself to blame if you find yourself in it. But this is not by any means true, unless we are to ask of certain players—and I fear these are the majority—to content themselves on some courses with playing shot after shot mainly for the purpose of safety. Any course merely laid out for the purpose of testing scratch players is likely to be a very bad course for players of less skill. In laying out a course one must have constantly in mind how various degrees of golfers may play it with pleasure. This is not an easy undertaking for an architect. It requires a lot of thought, but it can be done. On most holes the bunkers can be so placed as to force every player to do the best that is in him. The route for the poorer players may be somewhat longer and require more strokes in the play, but it will be a reasonably safe route which will not require them to dig out of some chasm, even when they have hit the best shots of which they are capable.

———————•◦•————————

Some inferior architects needlessly multiply their hazards. They work without any very clear idea as to the purpose of hazards, and sprinkle them here and there, sometimes with more ill effect than good. To place a bunker guarding the green on the right, and another bunker at the right of the fairway to catch a slice is to double the penalty for an error. The one bunker at the green would have been quite sufficient. Not infrequently one sees bunkers so placed as to prohibit good play. Bunkers behind the green often deter one from bold shots to the pin. Bunkers intended to punish a pull or a slice, sometimes prevent one from playing to the right or left of the fairway where the position may be ideal from which to play a second shot. The most absurd of all hazards are those which are placed to catch shots so bad that even had they found a good lie there would have been no possibility of an effective recovery. One of the most subtle and yet telling forms of bringing ruin upon the thoughtless golfer is to give him plenty of rope with which to hang himself. As an instance, suppose there is a certain tilt to the green such as is found at the fourteenth hole at St. Andrews. Give the headless golfer all the room he could desire at the right and if, in his madness, he finds his ball on that side of the hole, let him extricate himself if he can. The inferior architect would have tilted the green so that no one could have played the hole from the right and then sprinkled that side of the fairway with penal hazards so that no one would have had a chance to learn that a shot from that position was an impossible one. To make great holes, hazards need not be numerous. A few well-placed are quite sufficient to arouse any amount of lively interest and to call forth shots of which the best golfer may well be proud.

———————•••———————

Now and then I play on a very fine course where, for some unaccountable reason, the architect has seen fit to cut all his traps very deep, and their sides almost perpendicular. Little ladders lead one down to the flat bottoms. They resemble those pits made for our last resting place, and nearly every one entering therein should leave all hope behind. The most severe traps are those to punish wayward tee shots. And sometimes, when I find myself bunkered and manage by a hefty shot with the niblick to regain the fairway, I wonder if the architect does not work under the delusion that, if he can only make his penalties sufficiently severe, he will manage to end the era of tops, pulls, and slices. What an ardent reformer he must be! Unhappily he does not seem to be accomplishing what he is seeking. To be sure, he has put terror into the hearts of the delinquents, but instead of inducing them to lead a straightforward life he has made of them arrant and even more erring cowards. Penalties of a sort so severe that even the best of golfers will sometimes pick up his ball in despair destroy one of the most essential features of first-rate golf. No matter where the ball comes to rest in a hazard, there should be an opportunity for the player to make some recovery. Well played shots out of hazards are among the finest and most testing in the game. It is common to look with contempt on bunkers from which fine players will occasionally play a spoon. Certainly few opportunities of that sort should be offered; but when one does come it is a treat to see some great golfer play the shot. Is there any other stroke in the game requiring more precision than full shots out of sand? And is there any other stroke so brutish as an explosion—not to place the ball near the pin, but merely to get out of trouble?

By George C. Thomas:

In the building of hazards, there is as much need of foreseeing what will happen when the ball is trapped and the golfer forced to extricate it, as there is in visualizing any other part of golf construction.

In sandy or even somewhat sandy country, the play out of a hazard takes care of itself almost entirely; but in a land of clay, where sand is placed on top of it in hazards, the contours must be made so that the sand is in sufficient quantity always to be deep enough to keep the descending blade from contact with the hard ground below. For this reason gentle slopes which hold the sand are better than severe slopes from which it will be displaced; and a straight bank in front of the player is better than an easier grade on which the ball will be in shallow, ever moving sand.

———————

The size of traps should vary considerably; often a very small pot bunker on slightly raised ground is very valuable for orientation as well as for strategy, and small outcroppings of sand on natural or artificial mounds near a green are of much merit for the same reasons.

To stop a full drive, hazards will need more width as they are nearer the tee; certainly thirty feet of sand is the minimum, even when the hazard has some height. Sunken traps short of a green, and traps for orientation, especially with banks beyond them which are higher, may be made much smaller, particularly if the bank is fairly perpendicular.

Traps beyond greens to catch pitch shots which run over, need much less size than driving hazards, and usually less width than other green traps. The width and length of your hazards, the same as the width of your fairways and the location of your rough, should be made for the shot which is to be played on the hole, as well as for proper visibility. In addition, the finished production must conform with the adjacent ground for purposes of naturalness and beauty.

———————

Often a trap may be placed about which there is much comment when it first appears; but if that particular hazard is fair, if it gives an option to the high handicap man, such criticism will gradually die out, and eventually it will be commended. This applies most especially to the trapping of old holes, where the players are used to certain conditions, and where the new arrangement at first causes adverse criticism.

On a trap which I recently constructed, one player objected to it because he said: "If I make a bad drive, I cannot get on the green on my second shot." When everybody roared with laughter, it was realized that this very feature was the one which made the trap necessary and valuable.

Years ago there was a very canny Green Chairman, who placed piles of sand in the positions on his fairways where he proposed to make new traps, and after he had noted the result on the play of the hole and given the members a chance to express their opinions, he either built the hazards or took away the sand; and it was really quite surprising to note how many times he removed the sand, which shows the futility of placing new traps on old holes, unless there is a crying need for their presence.

The most necessary places for new traps are on courses where there is congestion, particularly where there is danger; and when this has been located and recognized, it is imperative for those in charge to make such changes and to give protection that will remove the peril.

By C.B. Macdonald:

I should like also to suggest that the construction of bunkers on various courses should have an individuality entirely of their own which should arouse the love or hatred of intelligent golfers. Rest assured such holes are far too complex for one's absolute condemnation or absolute approval. Bunkers of this character are much to be desired on any golf course.

Golf architects should make use of ground sloping in toward the bunkers as a means of enlarging the scope and peril of the bunkers. An appreciation of this is very valuable in constructing bunkers.

Always bear in mind that golf courses are not laid out for scoring competitions, and as long as a good player can get out in one stroke, either forward, backward, or to one side, that bunker is not unfair. The risk of going into a bunker is self-imposed, so there is no reason why a player should condemn a bunker as unfair. If there were not more or less luck in a game it would not be worthy of the name, and a risk should be taken commensurate with the gravity of the situation which brings out the ideal factor, luck, and raises it above a mere record breaking competition.

When one comes to the quality of the bunkers and other hazards we pass into the realm of much dispute and argument. Primarily bunkers should be sand bunkers purely, not composed of gravel, stones, or dirt. Whether this or that bunker is well-placed has caused more intensely heated arguments outside of the realms of religion than has ever been my lot to listen to. When there is a unanimous opinion that such and such a hazard is perfect, one usually finds it commonplace. Fortunately, I know of no classic hole that has not its decriers.

The eleventh hole at St. Andrews, which four of five golfers—a greater consensus of opinion than I have found regarding any other hole—concede to be if not the best, second to no short hole in existence, is berated vigorously by some able exponents of the game. At the last championship meeting at Hoylake, Mr. H.H. Hilton told me it would be a good hole if a cross bunker was put in and Strath closed. Heaven forbid!

To my mind, an ideal course should have at least six bold bunkers like the Alps at Prestwick, the ninth at Brancaster, Sahara or Maiden (I only approve of the Maiden as to bunkering, not a hole) at Sandwich, and the sixteenth at Littleton. Such bold bunkers should be at the end of a two-shot hole or a very long carry from the tee.

Further, I believe the course would be improved by opening the fairgreen to one side or the other, giving short or timid players an opportunity to play around the hazard if so desired, but, of course, properly penalized by loss of distance for so playing.

Other than these bold bunkers I should have no hazards stretching directly across the course.

Let the hazard be in the center or to either side or graduated in distance from the hole across the course. A very great number should be pot bunkers, particularly to the side; bunkers in which one can take a full shot with a wooden club are a travesty—some such bunkers as they have at Sunningdale.

CHAPTER 9

Greens

"Each green should be distinctive in character, and the type of shot required at the hole will largely determine what that is to be." – Robert Hunter

By C.B. Macdonald:

Putting greens to a golf course are what the face is to a portrait. The clothes the subject wears, the background, whether scenery or whether draperies—are simply accessories; the face tells the story and determines the character and quality of the portrait—whether it is good or bad. So it is in golf; you can always build a putting green. Teeing grounds, hazards, the fairway, rough, etc., are accessories.

———————

Regarding quality, nothing induces more to the charm of the game than perfect putting greens. Some should be large, but the majority should be of moderate size, some flat, some hillocky, one or two at an angle; but the great majority should have natural undulations, some more and others less undulating. *It is absolutely essential that the turf should be very fine so the ball will run perfectly true.*

A golf architect should endeavor never to construct what is known as a "trick green"; otherwise he will be suspected of being a card sharp. Don't seek an original idea in building a golf course. John La Farge somewhere has said if "an idea were an original one it is safe to say it would not be a good one."

By Robert Hunter:

There is nothing quite so vital in golf course construction as the proper placing and molding of the greens. Too much care cannot be taken to choose for them their permanent position. The building of greens is the most expensive item in course construction, and later changes here are sure to run into heavy charges. The changing of one green, which has been badly placed, may require the rearrangement of several holes. To place a green in some awkward position, demanding heavy costs for construction, is sometimes necessary; and it is far better to screw up one's courage in the beginning and build it there, even though it require a heavy outlay, than to place it in a position where it must prove unsatisfactory, and from which it must eventually be removed. The selection of sites for the greens requires both talent and practical judgment. In visiting a course where the greens have been ideally placed, there is a decided thrill of pleasure. The practical gain is often considerable in such cases, because much less construction is required where every natural hazard has been made to yield some value. On the other hand, it is often distressing to find almost ideal sites neglected, and a lot of money wasted in building greens which need not have been built had use been made of what nature had provided.

It is rarely advisable to place greens in deep hollows, on narrow ridges, or on steep slopes. Such positions are usually blind, and a shot to the green which the eye cannot follow is one of the least satisfactory in golf. Certainly one should avoid choosing blind sites for the one-shot holes. Too often in choosing the site of a green the designer has in mind only the length he desires for that particular hole, and some absurd position will be chosen because the tape-line has brought him to that point. That is a poor method to use in laying out a course. No doubt certain distances are desirable—some seem almost imperative—but where possible the position of the green should be chosen first. Then by lengthening or shortening the teeing ground, or by shifting it to the right or left, or by introducing a bend in the fairway, the desired length may often be obtained. Whatever may be the cause—bad judgment, the tape or some other equally silly reason—it is astonishing to see with what little care some greens have been placed. Quite ideal positions have sometimes been missed by only a few yards.

Of no less importance than the placing is the molding of the greens. Each green should be distinctive in charac-ter, and the type of shot required at the hole will largely determine what that is to be. Some greens may be quite flat, some of the saucer variety—although here one must give thought to the drainage—and some gently undulat-ing. Some should be wide, some long and narrow, while still others may be pear-shaped. The most satisfactory of all greens are often those which follow the natural lie of the ground, and which require no molding; although, of course, the soil should be carefully prepared for the grow-ing of good turf. For the most part these last are the kind of greens one finds in links land, and who could wish for better? It is advisable to do as little cutting and building as possible; but where these have to be done, strive to keep the elevations and contours harmonious with the immediate surroundings. Could anything be more offensive to the eye than some of the huge scars and angular erections which mark the sites of some greens? One of the objections to the growing practice of copying in all manner of country the greens of certain famous holes is the immense amount of building often required to give these greens a natural setting. Unless one is willing to spend large sums in molding large areas, most of these copies of famous holes will appear deformed and misplaced.

Without advising any club to adhere strictly and invariably to the following principles in the building of its greens, I believe they are worth careful consideration:

1. Construct every green so that surface water will readily drain from it, and be careful to see that the water is not carried off into a bunker. Preferably the drainage should be carried over the side of the green and not over its entrance. A slight slope will accomplish this. If the green lies so that a surrounding area is bound to drain over it, cut this drainage off by a grassy hollow.

2. At the edge of a green, sharp down slopes and abrupt rises are in most cases inadvisable, although gentle undulations may often be an attractive feature where one cannot hope to reach the green on the carry, or where it is desired to call forth some unusual shot.

3. Undulations on a few greens are most desirable, but ridges are almost always bad. They are usually ugly and it is difficult to grow good turf upon them. Furrows and ridges are bad types of undulations. "Pimples," "chocolate drops," and "carbuncles" are no less objectionable. The kind which should be molded is difficult to de-

scribe. Those found in the vicinity are often worth imitation. As sand blown up into little swells, or as the waves softly playing on the beach in long, graceful curves, so should be the undulations on a golf course.

4. Unless the contour of the ground makes it unavoidable, it will usually be wise not to build terraces on your greens. Where they are necessary the green must be large, and the incline from one level to another very gradual.

5. Let there be no place on the green proper where the ball will gain momentum after it is under way; but if this be unattainable, see that all such pronounced slopes be kept as far as possible from where the hole is to be cut.

6. On most greens about three-fourths of the area should be made available for cutting the hole. To change the cup frequently is necessary if the green is to be kept in perfect condition. A green may have many slight undulations, but it should also have many small areas which are almost flat. One should not be required to aim outside the circumference of the cup when making, let us say, a putt of three feet.

7. Greens should not be banked up so high at the back that every shot will hold; and, in the upkeep, greens should not be kept so soggy that every pitch must stop.

8. It is advisable that all slopes to the green and most of the slopes on the sides of bunkers should be made gradual so as to permit of their being cut by a triplex or horse drawn mower.

9. Each green should be built with a particular shot in mind. Its size, contours, bunkering, and opening should be considered in relation to that shot.

10. Not all greens should be built with the entrance coming in a line with the dead center of the fairway. Some

should be entered from the right and some from the left. Still others should have no opening at all—that is to say, they should be entirely surrounded by traps.

By George C. Thomas:

In the surface sketch of the greens themselves we need nothing but the slow, graceful roll, and they may be beautifully molded in undulations, and hardly ever should these be sharp. Roughly speaking, the peak of any rise on the green itself should have a base at least ten times its altitude. They are easily cut by the mower and do not dry out on top. In the making of these rolls, it is always necessary to have a general plan of drainage, for if you have a sunken valley with no outlet, the water will remain, and underdrainage be requisite.

In the forming of greens, beautiful modeling must conform to what a ball will do when it lands on a green from certain distances, and knowledge of what shot is necessary to reach it from strategic points, decides the contours of that green.

Rolls must not take up too much of the green. There must be space for the placing of the cup, and plenty of space for its changing; and the practical side of green building must consider drainage and subdrainage of the first importance. The green must not hold water; must not be flooded from higher levels, and should be so arranged that it does not drain into traps adjacent to it.

———————

When one comes to the areas of greens, the really difficult part of the proposition is faced, because greens are so much more significant in the play of the hole than any other equation; and there are so many things which affect the problem of the area of different greens, that the whole matter is most intricate. Here it is that the course builder must visualize with great accuracy the length of the stroke required, and the way various shots will act on reaching the green, and by foreseeing what the golfer and the golf ball will do, decide on the shape, extent and character of the green and its surroundings. He will give his opening, if any, the right width, and arrange for traps and fairways at the sides and beyond the green, as well as provide a green with necessary size and conformation for the reception of the ball.

While it is out of the question to make any arbitrary sizes for greens under the many varied conditions which will obtain, nevertheless, it is possible to give an idea of their correct dimensions by giving approximate measurements for their surfaces on flat holes. If these are used as a comparison, and the factors under any given condition considered in connection with them, it is believed that a guide will be supplied.

For a full wooden shot without carrying trap in front, a green should be not less than one hundred feet in length, with a minimum width of ninety feet, but one hundred and twenty-five feet for length, and one hundred feet for width would be better. The opening should equal this width; and where there is a carrying trap and no opening, add fifty feet of fairway back of the green; the carrying trap should be fifty feet short of the green. For all openings, if the sides of the same are built up, and slope toward the center, the width may be reduced.

Where your approach to such a green for a full shot is either uphill or downhill, the conditions must be considered; and the size of the green, the size of the opening, the distance of the carrying trap, if any, from the green; and the amount of fairway beyond the green must be calculated for the reception of the shots which it will take care of. In making these computations one should provide for the shot of the long man played to reach the green and secure par; and also for the shot of the short man. It is the way the balance of area is arranged for golf shots that a hole is properly or improperly constructed, and the strategy of the same either a success or a failure.

Taking up the sizes of greens for flat conditions for shots shorter than a full wood, the following areas are suggested as guides:

For a spoon shot or cleek, or a long iron to a green which is, roughly, from one hundred and eighty to two hundred yards, the minimum of the green should be ninety feet in depth, by eighty feet in width; but, preferably, it should be one hundred and ten feet by ninety feet; and carrying traps, if used, should be thirty feet short of the green, in which event give thirty feet of fairway behind green.

Greens built for the reception of a medium iron shot, the length of which is one hundred and sixty-five to one hundred and eighty yards, should be ninety feet in depth by seventy-five feet in width as a minimum—preferably, ninety-five by eighty-five feet; the carrying trap, if used, twenty feet short of the green, in which case give twenty feet of fairway behind green.

For greens to receive a jigger, mashie iron, or short iron, length from one hundred and fifty to one hundred and sixty-five yards, minimum size of the green should be eighty-five feet in depth by seventy feet in width—preferably, ninety by eighty feet; carrying trap, if used, fifteen feet short of the green, in which event give fifteen feet of fairway behind green.

Greens to receive long mashie shot, the length from one hundred and forty to one hundred and fifty yards, the minimum size of the green should be eighty feet in depth by sixty-five feet in width—preferably eighty-five by seventy-five feet; carrying trap, if used, ten feet short of the green, in which case give ten feet of fairway behind green.

For greens to receive long mashie niblick, length from one hundred and twenty-five to one hundred and forty yards, the minimum size of the green should be seventy-five feet in depth by sixty feet in width—preferably, eighty by seventy feet; the carrying trap, if used, five feet short of the green, in which case give five feet of fairway behind green.

For greens to receive a short mashie niblick, the length from one hundred to one hundred and twenty-five yards, the minimum size of the green should be seventy feet in depth by fifty-five feet in width—preferably, seventy-five by sixty feet; the carrying trap, if used, should be close to the side of the green with no fairway beyond.

CHAPTER 10

—•—

Greenkeeping

"There can be no first-rate golf courses unless the turf is of the right quality, nor can there be any great satisfaction in playing on courses, no matter how well designed, where the greens and fairways are not properly clothed and carefully groomed."
– Robert Hunter

By Robert Hunter:

Some day we shall have, I hope, books written upon grasses and greenkeeping, upon the methods and costs of construction, upon tools and maintenance and other problems connected with the building and administration of golf courses. Here my task is a limited one, and might be referred to as the anatomy of the links and their offshoots. Work in this field is still in its infancy, and the literature of the subject is limited to a few small volumes. Both in design and in upkeep the progress made in recent years is immense. There are some stunning things being done by the best men these days, but unhappily they are too busy to write about them.

SOIL

For many parts of the country there are now available the soil maps made by the government. Well-drained, slightly rolling country with a sandy soil or a deep rich loam is the ideal terrain for golf. Except in California, the clays should be avoided. On courses which depend upon the rainfall for their moisture, it is possible for only a short period of the year to have enjoyable golf on clay soils. In the wet season the fairways are muddy; in the dryer seasons they are hard as rock. After the heavy frosts of the winter have left the soil, the fairways must be ironed out with a heavy roller, and this must sometimes injure fatally the roots of the grasses. Artificial drainage will, however, greatly improve clay soils, and there are other ways of breaking up their too retentive nature. Clays are admirably suited, no doubt, for the growing of forage grasses, but they are rarely fitted for golf, or for the growing of turf best adapted to the game. I have excepted California from this generalization, because, on the coast at least, there is no frost to heave the ground, and on all the best courses the fairways are now watered during the dry season. Sprinkling supplies enough moisture to keep the clay fairways in excellent condition. But even in California the sandy soils and the loams are to be preferred. The grasses root more deeply there, and the player can force his irons into the turn without fearing that he will meet with mud or adamant. There are many difficult problems connected with producing good turf in areas of pure sand, and the experience of those in charge of Pine Valley and Pinehurst should be studied, but when the turf is once established the golfing conditions are ideal.

TURF

There can be no first-rate golf courses unless the turf is of the right quality, nor can there be any great satisfaction in playing on courses, no matter how well designed, where the greens and fairways are not properly clothed and carefully groomed. One might have a garden whose lines have been drawn by L'Enfant, but what would it be without plants and culture? Under certain conditions, tennis and even croquet become games of chance, and where this is true these sports will attract few. One often marvels at the control exercised by the expert over the action of a billiard ball. The best golfers are no less skillful. Indeed, the supreme joy in golf comes late and only to those who learn eventually to hit the ball in a manner which not only controls its length and flight, but even its action when it meets the turf. It must run, leap, or stop if the player has struck it properly. But no one can force the ball to act as he would have it unless the turf and the soil under the turf are suited to the game. The golf course architect who is himself an expert in the growing of grasses, or who has in his employ men who can be trusted to supervise the planting and care of the courses in their early stages, is the one to be preferred over all others, and especially over the many who run about the country selling their pretty plans, which too often, alas! mean little or nothing.

By George C. Thomas:
It would seem essential that every golf course should have its own nursery of bent grass, so that if greens do become invaded, it will be possible, by cutting the nursery sod very thin—approximately one inch in thickness—and

in long strips, to place it on the prepared surface of the green without keeping the same out of play for more than a couple of weeks. In other words, this thin-cut sod really acts like stolons, but its knitting is attained more rapidly than their growth.

If the soil on your course has considerable clay in it, it would be well to use a layer of sandy loam on top for the sowing of seed in the nursery for grass to be used in transplanting, because a sandy sod will move much more easily than the clay sod and without cracking; it will also be a better sod for your green.

————•●•————

Returning to the matter of different grasses, there have been a number of new developments since the old days, and we have gone through stages of using various grasses and considering them as the best for our greens and fairways. Originally we used red top, blue grass, and clover. Then we tried fescue and bent, the latter grass having for a time been planted by the vegetative or stolon method. Later on we reverted to the seed method with bent. We have also tried experiments with other varieties for the sides of our hazards and our rough.

Recently there has been a new bent developed by Dr. Carrier, of Oregon, which is known as Cocoos bent.

The old red top, and blue grass, and clover greens are undoubtedly inferior to the later developments. Bermuda, as a variety for greens, has lost its popularity, although there are some of these which gave very true putting surfaces, notably at the Los Angeles Country Club; and these greens also contain indigenous grass of California, resembling Poa annua.

At the Ojai Country Club in Ventura County, California, the greens are very fine. They are composed of fescue and red top, but they are somewhat inclined to be slow, although they seem well adapted to that climate of little frost in winter, and hot, dry summers; and, naturally, such greens are irrigated in that climate.

If the fairway is of Bermuda, and fescue is planted on the greens, it is invaded by Bermuda, and is also subject to mildew, especially in early fall.

If horse or cow manure is used on a green, it is very necessary to see that this manure does not contain ungerminated seeds of Bermuda, because under these conditions Bermuda will spread all over the green, and require most careful picking before it can be eradicated.

So far as may be decided, without a long test, the Cocoos bent is doing very well indeed; and as this is a creeping grass, it is more likely to ward off the incoming growth of other creepers, such as Bermuda. The bents are much superior for this reason. Metropolitan bent has been used with much success on some courses, but it would seem at this date that the Cocoos bent is very satisfactory.

The new La Cumbre course at Santa Barbara, the Bel-Air course near Los Angeles, and several other new courses are giving fine results with this Cocoos bent, and if this grass continues to stand up under usage, it will be very popular.

Bermuda fairways are very good. The mat of grass they produce is velvety and quite thick, on account of which it makes a very attractive fairway covering; but its scope is restricted to climates with little frost, and it is a terrible invader of surface occupied by the finer putting green grasses.

The virtue of Bermuda is its ability to quickly heal scars made on it by the divots cut by descending golf clubs; but from late practice Bermuda is on the wane, except in the very hottest and driest conditions.

Meadow fescue has been used by the Los Angeles Municipal Course on a terrain, some of which was originally pure, white sand, covered by a layer of good soil from four to six inches thick. Other parts of the course were heavy clay; and this grass has stood up well under the varied conditions, and very heavy traffic.

In certain places where greens have become hard, the use of a wire brush has been found beneficial each morning. This practice loosens the grass from the ground, and keeps it from being tramped flat, and a more receptive surface is afforded.

WATER SUPPLY

By C.B. Macdonald:

I have not touched upon one fundamental in golf course construction, and that is, the necessity of having an abundant supply of water with good pressure to sprinkle the fairway from one hundred and fifty to two hundred and seventy yards from the tee, and also the putting greens and the approach thereto. If the various courses in this country would water their fairway as above, you would hear very much less about two hundred and fifty to two hundred and eighty yard drives. Secondly, do not fail to have the low spots well drained.

By George C. Thomas:

In districts with very little water, I have seen landing places provided for the drive which were grassed and watered, and landing places around the green grassed and watered, the balance of the course, after clearing, being allowed to take care of itself; but under hot, dry conditions on clay land, this is an impossible proposition, because if the ground is not taken care of by seeding and watering, topped shots run tremendous distances on it, and a shot off the line sometimes secures greater distance than if played on the island landing supplied.

———————————

Even in the East it is found necessary to water many greens and some fairways, and such irrigation will become more prevalent; otherwise, unwatered courses in dry districts will fall into unpopularity.

In California an average eighteen hole course needs twenty-five miner inches of water as a minimum during the hottest part of the dry season. Twenty-five inches has two hundred and fifty gallons a minute flowing steadily all the time.

———————————

In considering area one must not neglect to make allowances for ground which floods, or which has poor underdrainage, because such territory is often out of play during rainy weather or in early spring.

Under such conditions many fairways are greatly improved by underdrainage and by protection from surface overflows.

Land which floods may often be guarded, and greens in such locations should be placed on the highest levels, or raised above low situations. On the other hand, certain ground cannot be made safe, and, as noted earlier in this text, land which floods badly should not be selected for golf courses.

Much damage may be done to the course by washouts; in some cases whole fairways have been lost and greens destroyed.

Where part of the property floods and the other portion is above storm water it is well to have a loop of holes in the low section, so that the high levels may be played as a unit during rainy weather.

Again, when high water is restricted in extent, the course may be planned so that overflow does not affect the play.

Many things enter into this problem; and local history and competent engineers should both be consulted on any location where this danger threatens.

CHAPTER 11

Ideal Holes

"In considering our ideal course, let us remember the value of diversity, and let us include in such a course as many varied shots, and the surmounting of as many different kinds of difficulties as is possible."
– George C. Thomas

By C.B. Macdonald:

Living in Chicago, I wrote an article, published in December, 1897, saying, in part:

"The ideal first-class golf links has yet to be selected and the course laid out in America. No course can be called first-class with less than eighteen holes. A sandy soil sufficiently rich to make turf is the best. Long Island is a natural links. A first-class course can only be made in time. It must develop. The proper distance between the holes, the shrewd placing of bunkers and other hazards, the perfecting of putting greens, all must be evolved by a process of growth and it requires study and patience."

Little did I dream I should live in New York and carry out this prophecy.

An ideal golf course must be controlled and developed by men who love and are devoted to the game without any possible emolument.

The fourth hole at the Lido I consider the finest two-shot hole in the world of golf, but fully ninety percent of golfers will have to play it as a three-shot hole. I absorbed the idea from the sixteenth hole at Littlestone, but the Littlestone Club never took advantage of the remarkable natural opportunity they had there of making a separate fairgreen among the dunes, where there was a perfect setting for it, a fairway set in the dunes some thirty to thirty-five yards in width and one hundred yards long, with a carry from the tee of one hundred and ninety to two hundred yards. Heaven knows when a player would get out of the rough if they didn't make this narrow fairgreen among the dunes, but once they did they had a wonderful driving iron or brassie shot to the green, which was on an eminence some fifteen to twenty feet above the fairway, with a deep bunker across the face of the green some forty yards from the hole. The bunker at Littlestone was about fifteen feet deep.

The charm of this hole at Lido is accentuated by the lagoon which encircles the entire fairway and which must be carried off the tee and also carried in the approach to the green, the back of the lagoon being about eighty yards short of the center of the green.

By Robert Hunter:

Ideal holes can, of course, be worked out on paper much easier than on the ground itself, although there are some holes in this country and abroad which are very near perfection. When I speak of an ideal hole I mean not only that it should be one of outstanding merit, but also one which all classes of players can enjoy, if they will only recognize their own limitations. I have recently seen a diagram of an excellent two-shot hole built by Donald Ross at Pittsford, New York, which seems to me not only simple in design but near to the ideal in its character. According to the ability of the player, the green can be reached in two, three, or four shots. Those who elect to take three or four shots have quite plain sailing, and should usually be able to reach the green without visiting a hazard. On the other hand, the man who intends to strike for the par of the hole has serious work ahead of him. He must not only carry some formidable hazards, but he must also have sufficient power to get beyond the last undulation. A high tee shot, a top, a hook, or a slice is almost sure to ruin any possibility of a four.

Two of the finest holes of the type I have been trying to describe are the two short ones at St. Andrews. It is difficult to construct short holes so as to make them testing for players of varying degrees of skill, and yet this is the chief merit of these remarkable holes. The eighth measures one hundred and forty yards and the green is quite large. About one hundred yards from the tee is an inoffensive looking ridge which is the making of this hole. It runs at an angle from a hollow of rough grass and bends to a deep pot bunker at the left edge of the green. The ideal ball would seem to be a high one with a touch of slice. This would carry the pot, but the green is hard and fast, and one wonders if he can put enough bite on the ball to stop near the cup. A ball with a slight pull over the ridge has at least twenty yards more leeway and, if the wind be not too strong, may be the better shot. The most dangerous but most effective shot would be a pitch-and-run. This should, if perfectly played, strike at the base of the ridge, bound over it and run close to the hole. What fascinating problems are presented here! The eleventh at St. Andrews is perhaps the best of all short holes. The green here is a bit smaller and the distance somewhat longer than at the eighth. The Cockle, or Shelly, bunker runs in from the right, about one hundred and ten yards from the tee. At the left of the green lies Hill bunker, and just beyond the green "the sandy horrows of Eden," while at the right is a small pot. Within the area of the green, on a line to its center, yawns Strath—a terrifying cavity from two to eight feet deep. Looking at this nest of hazards, one could sympathize with a champion, facing this hole in a critical round, if he were heard to pray: "O Lord, be merciful." Yet this hole may be well played, and often is well played by the local talent, with a putter.

Another great hole which illustrates my point is the famous Redan at North Berwick. Opinion is divided as to the others, but who disputes the claim made by the admirers of the Redan, namely, that it is the greatest single shot hole in the realm of golf? If imitation is the sincerest form of flattery, then the Redan surely deserves its fame. It has been copied again and again, and many replicas, such as they are, have been built in this country. It is a one-shot hole, measuring about two hundred yards. A huge bunker lies athwart the long narrow green which winds around to the left behind the hazard. Several bunkers lie in front of the tee, and others lie at the right of the entrance to the green. With a mashie, one could on almost any day play this hole in a four, but he who strikes for its par must execute perfectly one of three difficult shots. With a stiff head wind one may play either a long carry with the slightest touch of slice over the left end of the big bunker guarding the green, or a dead straight spoon shot directly over its center. If the golfer doubts his ability to play either of these shots, he may try a low flying ball to the right with a sharp pull, and run at the finish. No one of these shots is allowed much margin for error, and usually the slightest deviation in the line taken or in the action of the ball brings a severe penalty. Holes such as the two short ones at St. Andrews and this masterpiece at North Berwick make one hesitate in offering advice as to the best position for placing any bunker.

CHAPTER 12

————•◦•————

The Construction Process

"Do not let certain standards become an obsession. Quality, not length; interest, not the number of holes; distinction, not size in the greens—these things are worth striving for." – Robert Hunter

By George C. Thomas:

As a matter of information, the cost of a golf course is given in our text, but it will be understood that many things will affect an estimate for such work—the cost of clearing different kinds of country will vary; the amounts necessary to drain the course and to install the pipe lines are not fixed by any manner of means. The amount of earth which it is necessary to move affects the figures and it will be easily realized that many factors change the totals. Underdrainage on a heavy clay runs up to $10,000. However, the amounts given are those for an average course in California.

Clearing brush, trees, blasting rock, carrying
    sand and other necessary hauling $4,000

Grading of each hole, which includes the tee, traps, green, contours, covering hollows, over average ground at $1,000 a hole $18,000

Water system – The newest is hoseless on the fairways, with hose on the greens, because no system except hose has yet been worked out which is flexible enough for green watering, and which does not interfere with the play. The water system would include ditching not including rocky ground; the laying of the pipe, cost of the pipe itself, its fittings, and the back filling or covering of the pipe; the sprinklers and their fittings $24,000

Bent seed or bent stolons cost about $100 for 7,000 square feet, which would be an average green surface for 18 holes. $2,000

Sowing of the fairways with whatever fairway grasses were used (Bermuda would be about one-half the cost) $4,000

Labor of watering the course for six months, cutting, care of greens and fairways, top dressing, fertilizing for the same period; and other such necessary work as rock picking, weeding $20,000

Sand for the traps for an inland course . . . .   <u>$4,000</u>

Total construction cost. . . . .   <u>$76,000</u>

Such expenses would not include bridges, or any necessary grading of roads. Equipment of the best and most up-to-date character would approximate an outside figure of $5,000

PRECONSTRUCTION

Models must be used with the greatest care, for there are bad faults which crop up when you work with them. They must fit in their places with the utmost accuracy; levels must be taken with exactness, and the scale of the model be quite correct both horizontally and vertically. Even then, if you have not visualized it properly, and explained it clearly, it is likely to turn into a terrible object if you go away and let someone, who has not the three necessary qualifications of being an artist, and an engineer, and understanding golf strategy, try to reproduce it.

One of the most serious matters in working with a model is to place it correctly; not only must the green entrance face as desired, but the exact level of the flat base should be very carefully arranged. The slightest tilt in any direction will greatly affect the finished work. The proper placement of the model must be considered in connection with visibility and other practical necessities.

Nevertheless, where one cannot be on the ground during construction, a model accurately worked out, carefully checked and rightly placed by a man who knows the underlying principles of golf is very satisfactory.

The very opposite to this theory is that of one who works his ground before his eyes, molding it during its growth as he wishes it, and by this method producing the result with a minimum of effort. Such a man does not proceed primarily by means of a contour map as does the architect for houses and grounds. He commences to visualize as he molds his creation. Anyone who can do this, and do it well, has a great gift. His plan is an improvement over the original method of going at a green and "just making it," because he has ideals for which he is working, and he molds his green much as the other man molds the plasticine model, whereas in the old days when we started a green we had only hazy ideas of what we desired to produce. The whole theory of the fairway and strategy of that hole was not complete, and therefore our greens did not fit into the general scheme.

As for my own method, I find guessing levels very deceptive. I need a contour map and a few levels on the ground. My scale sketch of the plan of the hole works out for me the length of the shot from the tee, and the length and character of the shot to the green; and by my tests of carry with clubs and balls I know where the golf shots will go on the fairway later on. I work out my strategy for the entire hole. I visualize my green beforehand; I check such visualizations by levels. If I have an engineer in charge of the work who does not understand golf, I give him a model to work with in addition to the sketch of the hole; and I check his stakes after he has the green cross-sectioned and oriented on the ground. If I have a man in charge in whom I have absolute confidence, I need only give him a sketch to scale as a plan of the hole, and a sketch as to elevation. Then, as the green develops, I can see things to improve in it.

GRADING

Grading should next occupy your attention, and plans for all of it should be ready and passed upon, so that your working crews may proceed from one end of your course to the other in a sweeping advance. It should not be a question of going from No. 1 to No. 2, and so on. It should rather be a program that takes in the construction of adjacent greens, fairways, and hazards, and moves steadily across the property. In doing this see that a loop of nine holes may be played before the balance are ready.

All grading which includes the making of tees, fairway rolls, hazards, greens, and necessary drainage, must be entirely finished before seeding any unit.

In addition, roads for service through the grounds are very important; and these, and foot bridges, and other bridges must be built. Those used during construction should be planned to give access when the course is in play.

In years past, hazards were made after the fairway was in grass, the theory being that they were often misplaced otherwise, and that the course should be tried before their final positions were chosen.

Nowadays, it is found more desirable, for many reasons, to do grading, including trapping, before seeding, and the good sense of such practice is plainly apparent. First, it is a finished and not a patched job, and the drainage is more easily mapped as a whole if done at one time. Sand may be placed on the ground as the hazards are built, and it is not necessary to bring this in afterwards. Most important of all, the new fairways will not be cut up, bruised, and soiled by the unavoidable tramping of teams, and the dragging of implements across them if hazards are made before seeding, while the completion of the course by one operation is economical, and to play it after it is finished more pleasing.

WATER SYSTEM

By Robert Hunter:

Last, and not least under the list of experts, is someone qualified to lay out a proper system of drainage. With the contour map in hand he will not ordinarily find this work either long or irksome. Good turf in not obtainable without sufficient drainage. In some places a great deal of it must be done. One of the first operations in construction is the laying of the water pipes and the drains. Proper drainage in certain areas and soils may involve a large outlay. Some of it can be cheaply done by grassy hollows, and by the pitch of the greens, but most of it will require stone or tile. Excellent drains can be made out of stone, if that abounds; and, of course, it is better so to use it than to have to cart it away. Sub-irrigation of the greens has given remarkable results on some courses, and so has the underlaying of the greens with loose stone.

By George C. Thomas:

Underdrainage for fairways, for traps, and especially for greens, is a most important part of golf construction.

Its proper use is necessary in conjunction with the study of soil moisture. The differences found in soil and in rainfall make this subject very complex, while in districts without summer rain, and when it is necessary to give artificial sprinkling to the course, the matter must be handled intelligently.

On well-drained land, especially if the soil is light or sandy, and the subsoil not hardpan or heavy clay, under drainage is not perhaps obligatory, but even under such conditions there will be places on the course where it will be advantageous, and a green not properly drained will not grow good grass.

The Bulletin of the USGA Green Section gives a most careful handling of this subject, and various Engineering and Agricultural Experiment Station Bulletins are very valuable, although farm drainage is different from golf drainage.

The Cleveland District Green Section supplies a correspondence course for greenkeepers which is very thorough; and articles by the agricultural engineer, Wendell P. Miller, are comprehensive.

It would be advisable for the Committee in charge of construction of any course to take up this subject with their golf architect, and if he is not thoroughly conversant with it, arrangements should be made with experts to work with him.

The various factors entering into this question need expert advice.

SEEDING

When you come to the seeding of a course, you open the much mooted question of the best varieties of grass. The most satisfactory grass for fairways and for greens is still the source of unending argument, and as important as the selection of the kind of grass, is the preparation of the seed bed to receive it; and this applies particularly to the seed bed for the green.

In olden times there was the "shotgun green mixture," which contained different kinds of grass seed, on the theory that the one best suited to conditions thrived, and the others were crowded out or died.

A very keen golfer of Philadelphia, a Mr. Taylor, who was generally known as "Efficiency Taylor," tested many varieties of seed in carefully prepared beds, subjecting the grass germinated to the extreme of dry heat without water, and of dampness without sun; and by these trials he contributed very valuable data.

Furthermore, the seed beds which he finally decided upon as the most nearly perfect, and the variety of grass which he considered gave best results, were used on some of the greens of the Sunnybrook Golf Club, near Philadelphia, and elsewhere. These seed beds were complicated, and *Outing Magazine* described them in a contemporary article.

Without going very deeply into the details of these greens, it should be said that their general principles were complete underdrainage, a heavy body of plant food in the form of organic manure, placed above the drainage; a sufficient amount of friable soil; that is, a composition of soil which would not pack and thereby restrict the growth of grass roots later on.

It would seem that these considerations must be supplied on clay courses, as in Taylor's construction, but where there is light sandy loam, or sand, it is not always necessary to supply underdrainage; sometimes it is requisite to add heavier soil to retain moisture.

Recently I played over the Sunnybrook course, and found the greens there to be still in remarkably fine condition, their great virtue being that they did not dry out under heated circumstances and become hard; and that, in rainy weather, they were not too soggy.

It is advised that those who are constructing new courses should take up the matter of seed beds and grasses with the Department of Agriculture, as this Department keeps thoroughly in touch with this changing situation, and will give full and complete information on the best methods for various parts of the country.

CONSTRUCTING HAZARDS

By Robert Hunter:

Not only beauty but utility must be served when constructing hazards. Careful attention should be given to their shape, position, size—including depth—and the angle at which they are placed in the course. Certain common faults in construction make it worthwhile to emphasize the following points:

1. Be careful not to place bunkers where surface water will drain into them, or heavy rains wash the sand out of them. If such situations are so desirable that one is loath to give them up, protect them if possible by grassy hollows.

2. The inside contours of all depressions should be so molded that the ball will roll away from the faces of the cavity.

3. Where the banks of the bunkers rise above the level of the ground, make the outside slopes so gradual that a power mower can cut up to the edge of the depression.

4. See that the side banks are so built that no ball lying in the hazard will be unplayable. This means that there should be no sharp angles at the bottom or at the turn of the banks.

5. Little hillocks or abrupt rises may often be made into charming hazards by scooping out the faces and placing sand there.

6. It is advisable, but not always possible, to place hazards where they can be seen. Where a depression cannot be seen hummocks may often be seen, and they serve equally well as hazards.

7. All mounds should be built with a large base so that they will not appear high. The tops should, of course, not be

pointed, and their shapes should be as irregular as possible.

8. As a rule—there are exceptions—the bunkers through the fairway should be wide and shallow, and those about the green should be deep.

9. Ridges and hollows lying at the entrance of a green should not rise or fall abruptly, unless it is decided to force the players to run the ball or to pitch well up to the pin.

10. By depressing a large area around a bunker its efficacy is greatly increased, but if the ground rises at the entrance of a bunker many balls will leap over it unless it is made very wide.

11. Grassy hollows, mounds, and the banks of bunkers should be sowed with good seed and not allowed to grow wild, as otherwise they will become breeding places for weeds. The club which can afford to do so should plough up its rough and sow it also.

12. There are few natural hazards which do not require treatment to make them fitted for golf. No matter where the ball is found, one should be able to play it.

13. Easy access to and egress from all depressions should be arranged. To have to jump into pits and clamber up over their banks makes it impossible to keep them in good condition; and ladders should be used only as a last resort.

14. When it is found necessary, or it is thought advisable, to have traps directly back of the pin, they should, by all means, have sloping banks so that the ball will invariably run to the bottom of the trap. A grassy hollow or a shallow sand trap from which one can often putt is usually sufficient punishment for a straight shot which is a bit too bold.

15. Care should be taken to make bunkers of adequate depth and width. If they are too narrow the ball will often bound over them, and if they are too shallow the ball, which has not entirely spent its force at that point, will run through them. Wide, shallow bunkers are usually quite effective. I have even seen efficient hazards made by dumping large quantities of sand on portions of the fairway.

CONSTRUCTING GREENS

At the time the greens are being constructed, the entire area in that vicinity should be modeled. The approach, the traps, the mounds, and even the tee or tees for the next hole should be worked out as a unit. A considerable saving is usually made when the whole job is finished up in one operation. The soil taken from the bunkers can be used to build up the green, to erect attractive mounds, and to construct the adjoining tees. It should rarely be necessary to cart anything away from a golf course under construction. Even stone in great quantities can be used at the base of the greens to promote drainage, and, if covered with soil, as mounds which may be erected almost anywhere on the course not directly on the line of play.

By George C. Thomas:
Fortunately, the building of a green has considerable latitude. In some respects it is not a thing of minute exactness as to measurements. The slopes may vary. Even the levels may differ a few inches in height from the proposed plan without danger to the playing value, but woe be to one who does not understand and visualize the theory of the play of any given hole. He must provide each golfer

with a reasonable route of safety, and the green must properly receive shots played from the points on the fairway indicated by the strategy.

The drainage must be perfect; the putting surface faultless; the direct or indirect visibility supplied must be without flaw; and the green must have individuality. It is necessary for a problem to exist from tee to green—a problem to be solved differently by various players, and such green must be built by a man who has the ability to create. He must know in advance what he desires to produce, and must then produce it. There are many places where it is essential to grade a hole to secure distance, variety, or visibility, and again, grading will improve a hole to a great extent, under other conditions; but natural contours should be changed only where necessary, and many existing ones may be emphasized for superlative value.

RECONSTRUCTION

The rebuilding of courses is often severely criticized, and in many cases such censure is deserved; but it is well to remember that the gradual and continued improvement of golf courses has been brought about not only by the natural betterment of golf construction, but because of the increased efficiency of the golf ball, the playing value of which is more perfect, particularly with regard to its distance.

The advance in golf architecture, while progressing slowly, has, nevertheless, gone forward like other things, and lately the new handling of grasses and new varieties of grasses have also affected the situation. For these reasons, courses which were built some years ago cannot be expected to rank with the latest construction work. Therefore, there is often good reason for changes without censure to plans originally mapped out, and which produced the existing layout. On the other hand, there are courses which have not been properly constructed, and on which the strategy is not good. Furthermore, a club may decide to increase its playing arrangement from eighteen to thirty-six holes.

Under some circumstances, there is the necessity of continuing play during the period of change; and with the aid of temporary greens and tees this may generally be accomplished. Oftentimes a new loop of holes constructed over new territory will take the place of other parts of the course to be changed.

Present day methods entail a different type of architecture to that employed several years ago in a great many cases, although often the old holes may be remodeled without much expense, and thereby fit in properly with the new parts.

It is possible to add acreage to a congested tract and improve the old ground by lessening the number of holes thereon, and secure additional character over them, possibly by dodging hills, lengthening holes which are too short, and by various means increasing the total yardage, if such is desired.

These problems are very confusing. It is really more difficult to reconstruct an old course than to lay out a new one, because the question frequently arises as to what should be discarded and what retained. One feels that every time one eliminates something, it may be possible that sufficient value, over and above what exists, is not obtained in the new construction. Very few of the old holes can be played as they stand, but undoubtedly the greater part of their fairways are valuable, and only the very finest of them should be kept intact.

————•—————

In the remodeling of a course, the architect must be in complete sympathy with the Chairman of the Green Committee and the policies of the club. He must approve of what is to be done before he can properly execute the wishes of the organization. When this cooperation exists, the work is a pleasure, and I have been fortunate in having been associated with Chairmen who knew golf and who were of the greatest assistance. On one of the last courses which I helped to reconstruct, I considered the Chairman had the utmost understanding of golf architecture, and the result was very successful.

When there is adverse criticism in rebuilding a course, it usually occurs when the work is undertaken by the man who formerly looked after the upkeep, and nearly always such workers are unable to understand the difference between their previous jobs of upkeep and their new ones of construction, even though they have done some little work in the making of traps and minor alterations.

It is very difficult for the architect to produce the same results with unskilled labor as he is accustomed to create with men who understand his methods and have produced former conceptions.

Reconstruction should be handled by the same type of labor which builds courses, and if the architect cannot have the construction men who have worked with him before, or others whom he can depend upon to carry out his plans, it would be better not to attempt the work. New traps and new tees are one thing, the proper molding of greens an entirely different matter.

Therefore, do not try reconstruction without expert advice, and without giving your expert a proper chance to produce what both you and he desire.

Frequently it would be wise for an organization to consider the sale of the property, and the purchasing of a new tract, where an up-to-date course can be built, rather than to attempt the reconstruction of an old course, especially if such is not situated on terrain which will give the most advantageous results.

Nevertheless, on numerous occasions I have endeavored to bring this opinion before committees of clubs, and found it very hard to impress them with the hopelessness of reconstructing a course of the highest character from mediocre possibilities.

If the proposition is for but a small membership, and great length is not desired, an old course, unless on very bad ground, should be reconstructed with success.

However, every problem is different and must be solved to the satisfaction of those who own the property, and the architect must look at their point of view; but on the other hand, he should present to them what they will secure if they go ahead with remodeling.

While it is necessary in the remaking of old-fashioned courses to remodel, this should not be done so that the membership of a course, which has had rather easy play, will be under the necessity of making long carries from tees and to greens on the new layout, unless such changes are thoroughly understood. The theories for the building of a new course apply with equal force to the remade proposition.

CHAPTER 13

———◄•►———

Overseeing Construction

"It was imperative I secure an associate, one well educated with wide engineering capabilities, including surveying, companionable, with a fine sense of humor, but above all, earnest and ideally honorable. Such a man I found in Seth J. Raynor." – C.B. Macdonald

By George C. Thomas:

As your construction advances, your work must be constantly supervised, and the OK of your architect insisted upon before any green is seeded. It is necessary that contours should be checked, so that there is no possibility of the sinking of any part of a green, mounds, and so forth; and that all raised portions have been solidly packed, for it is remarkable how rain will shrink rolls if they are not carefully made. When such an event takes place, the appearance is nothing like that desired.

———◄•►———

Again and again, during course construction, I have been asked to let some employee of a club carry out the work, and whenever I have acceded to such requests, I have had the greatest difficulty in carrying out my plans properly. This is not intended in any way to reflect on the men who have done this work, but is rather to avoid subjecting them to a task for which they are not qualified, and which it is unfair to ask them to do.

No matter how good a man is for supervising a course, he may not have the golfing knowledge, or the artistic sense, or the engineering education to carry out golf course construction. The golf architect should be made responsible for contours; for every detail in the construction of the course. His contract should be made so that he either supervises this work himself, or supplies a competent foreman who is responsible in his absence. In this latter event, the architect should inspect the job a stated number of times. You may spend more money by using his men than by trying to get him to work with yours at the time of the building, but eventually you will save if you make him entirely responsible, and have his OK, especially before any seeding is done.

After the plan of the course is accepted, do not change it and hamper the architect by letting your Green Committee, or anyone else, supervise the work and take responsibility away from the architect, who may very properly say afterwards that errors which cropped out in the construction were caused by the men whom you had placed in charge.

By all means have the work watched, but make the architect responsible. There are some Green Committees who can build a golf course; there are many more who cannot do so.

SETH RAYNOR

By C.B. Macdonald:

After the National Golf Links of America had gained more or less of an international reputation I was approached and importuned by various friends in different parts of the country to make plans for constructing golf courses for them, they little dreaming the time and work this involved. This labor did not pall on me at first, for I was flattered and happy to feel I was attaining the much dreamed of objective, architecturally constructing classical golfing holes that would challenge criticism throughout the golfing world. I was contented with the knowledge that I was really contributing something to American Golf and at the same time had the pleasing sense of gratifying my more intimate friends.

In accomplishing this end it was imperative I secure an associate, one well educated with wide engineering capabilities, including surveying, companionable, with a fine sense of humor, but above all, earnest and ideally honorable. Such a man I found in Seth J. Raynor.

Seth Raynor was born in Suffolk County in 1878 and settled in Southampton as a surveyor. Employing him to survey our Sebonac Neck property, I was so impressed with his dependability and seriousness I had him make a contour map and later gave him my surveyor's maps which I had brought from Scotland and England, telling him that I wanted those holes laid out faithfully to those maps. For three to four years he worked by my side. He scarcely knew a golf ball from a tennis ball when we first met, and although he never became much of an expert in playing golf, yet the facility with which he absorbed the feeling which animates old and enthusiastic golfers to the manner born was truly amazing, eventually qualifying him to discriminate between a really fine hole and an indifferent one.

When it came to accurate surveying, contours, plastic relief models of the land, draining, piping water in quantity over the entire course, wells and pumps, and in many instances clearing land of forests, eradicating the stones, finally resulting in preparing the course for seeding, he had no peer.

In 1911, Roger Winthrop, Frank Crocker, Clarence Mackay, and other Locust Valley friends wished me to build the Piping Rock Golf Club course. I found they wanted a hunt club as well as a golf club. Some of the leading promoters thought golf ephemeral and hunting eternal. Consequently, I had my troubles. The first nine holes were sacrificed to a racetrack and polo fields. However, all's well that ends well, for today golf is King and Queen in Locust Valley. I employed Raynor on this job. It would have been difficult to accomplish it without him. There was too much work and too much interference.

Next, James A. Stillman's friends lassoed me to lay out a golf course in Sleepy Hollow. It seemed an almost impossible task to carry through; because we were told that William Rockefeller would not consent to any trees being cut down or removed. I was almost inclined to throw up the task. However, at a meeting which Cooper Hewitt, Jim Whigham, and I had with William Rockefeller and Frank Vanderlip, I was given a free hand. This was a hard task for Raynor in appalling summer heat.

Next came the St. Louis Country Club, then the White Sulphur Springs layout, and then finally came the colossal task of the Lido at Long Beach. By this time Raynor had become a post-graduate in golfing architecture, and since

1917 built or reconstructed some one hundred to one hundred and fifty courses, which I have never seen. The Mid Ocean Club, the Yale Golf Club, the Links Golf Course, the Gibson Island Golf Course, the Deepdale, and the Creek Club were the only ones I gave any personal attention to after 1917.

Raynor built courses in every climate, in Puerto Rico, the Sandwich Islands, three or four in Florida, two in California, and numberless elsewhere. He was a world builder. I had given him all my plans and only occasionally was I asked for advice.

Sad to relate he died ere his prime at Palm Beach in 1925 while building a course there for Paris Singer. Raynor was a great loss to the community, but a still greater loss to me. I admired him from every point of view.

APPENDIX A

Selected Courses by C.B. Macdonald

Includes collaborations and redesigns:
- Chicago Golf Club, Illinois
- Course at Yale, Connecticut
- Creek Club, New York
- Downers Grove Golf Club, Illinois
- Greenbrier – Old White Course, West Virginia
- Lido Golf Club, New York
- Mid Ocean Club, Bermuda
- National Golf Links of America, New York
- Piping Rock Club, New York
- Sleepy Hollow Country Club, New York
- St. Louis Country Club, Missouri

APPENDIX B

Selected Courses by George C. Thomas

Includes collaborations and redesigns:
- Bel-Air Country Club, California
- Fox Hills Golf Course, California
- La Cumbre Country Club, California
- Los Angeles Country Club, California
- Los Angeles Municipal Golf Courses, California
- Marion Golf Course, Massachusetts
- Ojai Country Club, California
- Palos Verdes Golf Club, California
- Red Hill Country Club, California
- Riviera Country Club, California
- Saticoy Country Club, California
- Saticoy Regional Golf Course, California
- Spring Lake Golf Club, New Jersey
- Stanford University Golf Course, California
- Whitemarsh Valley Country Club, Pennsylvania

APPENDIX C

Selected Courses by Robert Hunter

Includes collaborations and redesigns:
- Cypress Point Club, California
- Green Hills Country Club, California
- Meadow Club, California
- Mira Vista Golf and Country Club, California
- Monterey Peninsula Country Club, California
- Northwood Golf Club, California
- Pebble Beach Golf Links, California
- Sharp Park Golf Course, California
- Valley Club of Montecito, California

ABOUT THE PUBLISHER

Coventry House Publishing is a traditional publisher of adult fiction and non-fiction titles. Founded in Dublin, Ohio in 2012, we're beginning a long tradition of serving readers and authors across the country, one book at a time.

We pride ourselves on the quality, meaningful work we publish. Our primary genres of focus include business & economics, sports & recreation, education & social science, and fiction & entertainment. Please visit our website, www.coventrybooks.com, for more information about our featured books and authors.

INDEX